The Distribution of Authority
in Formal Organizations

— The Distribution of Authority
in Formal Organizations —

GENE W. DALTON
Associate Professor of Organizational Behavior

LOUIS B. BARNES
Professor of Organizational Behavior

ABRAHAM ZALEZNIK
*Cahners-Rabb Professor
of Social Psychology of Management*

HARVARD UNIVERSITY
DIVISION OF RESEARCH
GRADUATE SCHOOL OF BUSINESS ADMINISTRATION
Boston

1968

ABSTRACT

The Distribution of Authority in Formal Organizations

This volume is the first of two studies of engineers and scientists in formal organizations by Professors Zaleznik, Barnes, and Dalton. It concentrates on the impact and developing effects of a series of changes in organizational structure and arrangements in a research and development center of a larger parent organization. As such, it addresses itself to the related issues of authority and social change.

The book is the third in a series of studies which have been proceeding under the direction of Professor Zaleznik. The items of this series are related by a common interest in the exploration of several major dimensions of organizational research: (1) the process of role taking and its relationship to personality; (2) the dynamics of interpersonal behavior, especially in the setting of the small group; and (3) organizational structure, particularly as it establishes the constraints, or the initial "givens," around which role and interpersonal behavior develop.

The authors of this new study are Gene W. Dalton, Associate Professor of Organizational Behavior, Louis B. Barnes, Professor of Organizational Behavior, and Abraham Zaleznik, Cahners-Rabb Professor of Social Psychology of Management, at the Harvard Business School.

This study addresses itself to two related issues of increasing importance to management: authority and change. Recent years have witnessed unprecedented challenges to existing authority in organizations, accompanied by demands that the institutions themselves be changed. At the same time, organizational leaders have become increasingly concerned with the process of revitalizing their organizations to cope with the rapid social and technological developments in their environment. The changes they introduce almost inevitably alter the existing patterns of authority and power, and there is increasing evidence that responses to management's change efforts cannot be anticipated or even explained without examining their impact on the authority structure. There is an increasing need, therefore, to examine these issues together.

This book is, in one sense, an empirical and a theoretical study of authority as one dimension of the formal organization structure. It uses as a focus, as well as a point of departure, the experience of one organization in which the top executive sought to alter the formal organization. It analyzes his actions and the responses of others in terms of their effect on the authority structure. But it is also a study of organizational change. The actions taken by the executive received varying responses among individuals within different groups in the organization. An analysis of these actions and their effects illuminates some of the critical factors in the introduction of change.

Two types of research design and methodology are combined in this study. The first is that of a case study that analyzes one situation over time, thus permitting a view of organizational dynamics. The unit chosen for study was the development center for a large organization which operated in an industry characterized by rapid technological change. During the beginning of the period studied, a new director was appointed. He became concerned about recurrent project delays and the need for greater identification with project success among members of the staff. His steps to cope with these problems through a structural reorganization designed to "move decision-making downward" are examined in some detail. The second is that of a natural experiment with an emphasis on control and measurement of variables to the extent that these were possible in a field setting. Before any of the changes were announced, the investigators were allowed to assess the operations and attitudes at the Center in order to establish a base-line against which subsequent measures could be compared. These measures were administered both to the groups included in the reorganization and to a "control" group not involved. Then a year after the reorganization was put in effect, a second set of questionnaires and interviews was used to measure the effects of change.

Although the director had hoped that the reorganization would have a positive effect on all the members of the experimental departments, the measured results indicated that the changes in behavior and attitude were not uniform and were closely related to changes in authority. For two groups in the experimental departments, the Junior Managers and the Senior Scientists, the structural changes had brought both greater autonomy and an increased opportunity to exercise authority. Both these groups reported increased personal productivity and satisfaction. The Senior Managers and the Junior Scientists in these departments, on the other hand, experienced a relative reduction in authority. Their contact with others who made decisions had been curtailed; they were now less likely to be present in settings where decisions were made; and men whom they had influenced before now listened to others. These two groups were consistently less responsive to the aims of the program and less positive in evaluating its effects.

Response also varied with anticipated trends in the distribution of authority. One of the effects of the reorganization had been to force greater reliance on professional authority as opposed to position-based authority than had been done in the past. Anticipation of a continuation of this trend divided the men along functional lines in their attitude toward further change. Regardless of the degree to which individuals had already gained or lost authority, Managers as a whole were in favor of a halt to the changes, or at least to a reduced rate of change, while Scientists favored an acceleration and an extension of the program.

Unfulfilled expectations appeared to have the same effect as actual loss. Heightened expectations, triggered by the actual changes, resulted in dissatisfaction with superiors and a greater tendency to consider leaving the Center among respondents whose authority and influence remained unchanged.

Utilizing these findings and contrasting them with other empirical studies of organizational change, the authors explore some of the factors that tend to characterize successful efforts to change behavior in organizations. Tension as a prior condition of change is examined, along with the power of the person proposing the change. Even when tension for change is present and a change originates from a powerful and respected source, the analysis suggests that the individuals involved are unlikely to maintain the changed attitude or behavior unless (1) the goals and objectives toward which they are working become increasingly specific and concrete; (2) the relationships which reinforce their former attitudes and behavior are altered or severed, and they establish new relationships supportive of the change; (3) their sense of self-esteem is heightened in the process of change; and (4) they internalize the content of the motive for change.

The authors agreed that differences among them in interpretation or conclusions would be documented and shared with the reader rather than obscured or avoided. Therefore in the last two chapters, where the authors summarize the study and explore some of the important issues raised by the findings, the reader will find differing and sometimes opposing views expressed. One issue concerns the question of rationality in the structural design of organizations. It is suggested that formal organization, like informal organization, has both rational and nonrational components. A serious question is posed as to whether, at the level of overall organization planning, a rational basis can be found for choosing one design over another. Are decisions at this level inherently nonrational in character? A related issue concerns the relationship between the manifest intent of a given change and its latent effects in terms of the resolution of problems of power and authority. In what sense are the arguments which are advanced to support a given change actually rationalizations to support a predetermined course of action which has its roots in latent social and psychological forces? A final issue concerns the bases for assessing changes in power within an organization. Will increases in the power of one party inevitably be experienced as a relative loss by another, or are there conditions under which gains in the total amount of power become salient rather than relative gains and losses?

(Published by Division of Research, Harvard Business School, Soldiers Field, Boston, Mass. 02163. xiii + 229 pages. $6.00. 1968)

FOREWORD

THIS VOLUME, *The Distribution of Authority in Formal Organizations*, is the third in a series of four related studies which have been proceeding under the direction of Professor Zaleznik. The other two, *Role Development and Interpersonal Competence* by David Moment and Abraham Zaleznik, and *The Executive Role Constellation* by Richard C. Hodgson, Daniel J. Levinson, and Abraham Zaleznik, were published by the Division of Research in 1963 and 1965 respectively. The final volume is expected in 1969. The items of this series are related by a common interest in the exploration of three major dimensions of organization research: (1) the process of role taking and its relationship to personality; (2) the dynamics of interpersonal behavior, especially in the setting of the small group; and (3) organization structure, particularly as it establishes the constraints, or the initial "givens," around which role and interpersonal behavior develop.

This latest volume is a study of the impact and developing effects over a two-year period of a series of changes in organizational structure and arrangements in a research and development center. It utilizes the approach of a field experiment to assess the effects of these changes on the productivity and satisfaction of the professional personnel engaged in research and development work. The research focuses on a newly promoted director — a scientist-executive — and his organization of some 150 engineers, scientists, and managers engaged in technical development work for the larger parent organization. The director introduced a series of ideas designed to alter the authority make-up of the center in an attempt to improve the effectiveness of the organization. These changes are described as structural changes in that they involve shifts from one set of task-people relationships to another. Because of the two-year period of the study, it was possible to develop, although crudely, a "before-after" and "experimental-control" study design. In this book the researchers not only present an account of how this effort in organizational influence began, developed, and continued over the two-year period; they also analyze and interpret their observations, in part jointly and in part separately.

This project, like the others in this series, has involved a collaborative effort on the part of two or more researchers. In this instance the three authors worked together in planning and designing the research, and then Professor Dalton did the field work for the study. He and Professor Barnes prepared the initial analyses and working papers, and Professor Dalton wrote the initial drafts of Chapters I through V. All three authors participated in reviewing and revising early drafts, and Professor Zaleznik took the responsibility for writing a concluding chapter and for the final revisions and editing of the earlier chapters.

In my experience, most instances of fully collaborative research involve elements both of strength and of weakness. Major gains from collaboration seem to arise at the design, data gathering, and analysis stages; and major problems and differences frequently arise in attempting to reach final conclusions, interpretations, and implications of the study. This project was no exception; there were both gains and strains in the collaboration. It became impossible to achieve agreement among the three authors on a concluding chapter and on specific points in earlier chapters. Because Professor Zaleznik had carried out the final revisions and editing, the manuscript submitted for publication reflected his views in most instances where there were differences among the authors. Because Professors Dalton and Barnes believed that the manuscript did not adequately reflect their views, they were given the opportunity to write a separate concluding chapter, to make additional revisions to Chapter V, and to append footnotes of comment to particular points in other chapters which would enable them to express major differences from the manuscript as edited by Professor Zaleznik.

The volume as published is thus somewhat unusual in having two concluding chapters and other differences among the co-authors forthrightly expressed. Professor Zaleznik is the author of Chapter VI. Professors Barnes and Dalton are co-authors of Chapter VII, and they undertook the final revision of Chapter V. Professor Zaleznik did the final editing of Chapters I through IV, but there are a few footnote comments of differences by Professors Dalton and Barnes in Chapters I and III.

Finally, may I express for the authors and the School our appreciation of the financial support which made the study possible. Allocations to support the project were made from a grant of the Ford Foundation to support research in organizational behavior, from gifts by The Associates of the Harvard Business School, and from the income of the B. F. Goodrich Company Endowment for Research in Memory of David M. Goodrich. We are grateful for this generous support of research at the School.

BERTRAND FOX
Director,
Division of Research

Soldiers Field
Boston, Massachusetts
June 1968

ACKNOWLEDGMENTS

WE ARE singularly indebted to the director, the managers, the scientists, and the engineers of the organization disguised here as the Nampa Center. It was their deep commitment to the process of inquiry which made this study possible.

We are grateful to Bertrand Fox, Director of Research, who spent many hours helping us to find a format which was designed to clarify rather than obscure the issues involved in the phenomena under scrutiny in the book. The contribution of his sure hand in guiding the efforts of the Division of Research found ample demonstration in this study.

The careful work of Ruth Norton in moving the manuscript into published form can be appreciated only by those who have worked with her.

We should also like to acknowledge our debt to our secretaries, Ann Beale, Jane Edwards, Sandra Narot, Jean Neal, Mary Redgate, Ann Reiger, and Marjorie Van Leuvan, for the countless ways in which they have contributed to the completion of this study.

We also wish to thank Dean George P. Baker and Associate Dean George F. F. Lombard for their support and for making it possible for us to devote part of our time to this research.

While we are grateful to all the above for the many ways in which they have contributed to this study, we accept full responsibility for the work and contents of this book.

G. W. DALTON
L. B. BARNES
A. ZALEZNIK

TABLE OF CONTENTS

LIST OF TABLES

LIST OF FIGURES

CHAPTER I

Formal Organization in Research and Practice

THE THEORY of formal organization structure stands in a paradoxical position both in research and in its practical applications. When managers try to alter behavior they almost instinctively reach first for a new formal structure. As a result, action often follows popular trends. There are periods, for example, when decentralization is the popular theme in management practice, only to be followed by a reverse trend toward centralized planning and control. But aside from current trends in practice, the connections between an organization's problems and the remedies applied in changing the formal structure often remain tenuous, notwithstanding rationalizations which appear in support of a particular program.

In academic circles the condition is just as confused. New theories appear claiming support from scientific research. The research is usually so conditional, if not thin, as to make unwarranted the blanket advocacy of programs and ideologies of organization and management.§

PUBLISHER'S NOTE: See the Foreword for an explanation of the signed footnotes.

---

§ DALTON-BARNES COMMENT: In our view, the designing of organizations reflects more than the following of "popular trends." In addition, though much research remains to be done, a blanket indictment of current research also seems unjustified. Task, technology, and environmental certainties seem to be important variables in the designing of organizations. An instance of such rational design flows from computer technology which has resulted in the centralizing of accounting practices, purchasing procedures, production control systems, manpower planning, etc., in order to utilize the computer's capacity and for standardization purposes. Similarly, research findings on organizational design are indeed conditional and do not warrant

There is no explicit theory of organization structure which can explain, let alone predict, the relationship between structural inputs and outcomes such as performance, productivity, and satisfaction. At the present stage of research there is still a great deal of work to be done in defining, describing, and measuring the variables under study as well as their interrelationship.

Formal organization structure as a concept screens many social-psychological variables. It is at the outset a symbol intended to represent the distribution of authority among the occupants of positions. This distribution can be expressed only in relative terms, comparing one position with another at a given point in time or the same position at different times.

The formal structure also defines areas of accountability in establishing the zones of performance which fall within the competence of a position. One consequence of accountability is the presumption that an individual who occupies a position will be appraised according to certain standards of individual and group performance.

In establishing accountability, the structure also provides the range of relationships operative for a given position. This range, sometimes called a role set, places individuals in varying degrees of proximity to one another and gives substance to the play of expectancy. It also creates the formal groups which help define membership and relate to individual identity.

Besides symbolizing authority, accountability, and range of relationships which make up the organization, the formal structure also embodies the contract which brings individuals to work. In this sense, the structure encompasses a motiva-

blanket advocacy of any practice, but the same statement may be made of any social and most physical science inquiries. In fact, it is the search for these determining variables (e.g., type of task) which now provide some of the most promising research leads on organizational design. See Chapter VII for further notes on this issue.

tional set which makes it possible for people to enter into exchange within the organization and with the individuals in it. But besides creating a motivational set, the organization itself becomes activated as members pursue their interests and give expression to their motives.

It is a commonplace to observe that the formal organization chart does not tell the whole story about the shape and dynamics of an organization. This is true, not only because of the so-called informal organization, but because of the inherent complexity underlying formal organization itself. The problem for research is not simply to demonstrate the relationship between formal and informal organizations as global and opposing structures, but in addition, to understand what lies behind formal organization structure as it activates social-psychological process within and among individuals.

This book is both an empirical and a theoretical study of authority, one of the significant dimensions which make up formal organization structure. It uses as a focus, as well as a point of departure, the experience of one organization in which the top executive altered the formal organization structure as an instrument of change. From his frame of reference, the change consisted of "flattening" the organization structure and redefining the relationships within and among work groups. In effect, the top manager eliminated selected management positions and altered the authority of others. Work group supervisors as project leaders consequently had increased authority and widened zones of competence.

The general objective in "flattening" fits in with current notions of decentralization and power equalization: where the gap between degrees of authority from the top to the bottom of the organization decreases, the motivation to work hard increases and will be reflected in measures of productivity and satisfaction.§

---

§ DALTON-BARNES COMMENT: There is evidence that "flattening an

Equalizing authority can be accomplished in a variety of ways. The most direct is to alter the formal organization structure and its job definitions. When this occurs in a real organization, the situation is ripe for a research study. The authors of this study utilized this natural experiment in altering the distribution of authority for two purposes: (1) to clarify the meaning of authority as a concept and a variable in formal organization structure; (2) to measure the effects of equalization or "flattening" on work relationships, performance, and job satisfaction.

THE RESEARCH SETTING

Chapter II will present in considerable detail the case history of the Nampa Development Center leading to the program to alter the distribution of authority; but there are some special features of this organization which if presented now will increase appreciation of the relevance of the experiment which provided the raw material for this research.

Briefly, the Nampa organization operated as an applied research and development center in one division of a large corporation. The corporation as a whole competed with a sophisticated technology in which new products as an outgrowth of research and development were crucial elements for corporate success.

The industry itself provided many jobs for highly trained engineers and scientists and the corporation had its share of professional employees. The Nampa Center alone employed about 180 professionals, all of whom participated in this research.

The chief executive of the Nampa Center had held a series

organization" and "power equalization" are independent phenomena (Bell, 1967; Blau, 1968). They may complement each other but should be considered separately. In the Nampa study, task-environment, exchange mechanisms, and power-dependency relationships all seem to relate to the organization's structure in more critical ways than does power equalization.

of technical and administrative posts and had performed capably in these positions. Corporate management promoted him to the directorship of Nampa. In taking this job, the new Director defined it as simply to increase research and development output. The means he chose were basically the alterations in structure which will be described in detail in Chapter II.

RESEARCH DESIGN

This study combines two types of research design and methodology. The first is the case study in which intensive analysis of one situation over time permits a view in depth of organizational dynamics. The second is the experiment with its emphasis on control and measurement of variables.

The Director of Nampa decided on his objectives and the means for achieving them apart from any considerations of management research. He agreed, however, to alter the timing of the changes in structure to help the researchers plan a field experiment which would be as close to a controlled experiment as possible in a natural organization.

The researchers utilized several methods of gathering data from the various sources in the organization. They studied existing records and conducted a series of interviews with some of the managers and engineers. They attended a number of regular meetings and recorded what went on. Based on the information gained from these various sources, a series of questionnaires were designed and administered [see Appendix A] to establish measures of base line or "before-change" attitudes. Fifteen months later the "after-change" measures were provided by a second set of questionnaires, interviews, and observations. The comparisons of the two measures form the basis for evaluating the effects on performance and attitudes of the new distribution of authority. In addition, certain groups remained outside the planned change and served as comparison groups. We hesitate to call these strictly control groups because of the difficulty in isolating them from the involvement in a significant change in organization structure. Nevertheless, comparing groups which were directly altered with groups not directly changed serves a useful analytical purpose.

Both sets of comparisons described above can be summarized in Figure 1, which presents the logic of the experimental approach in this study.

FIGURE 1

THE STRUCTURE OF THE RESEARCH DESIGN

	Before change	After change
Change Groups	A_1	A_2
Comparative Groups	B_1	B_2

Chapter IV will present quantitative data following the four-cell structure of the research design illustrated in Figure 1.

RESEARCH QUESTIONS

Chapter III presents a theoretical discussion of the concept of authority and its relationship to formal organization structure. It deals in particular with clarifications concerning the sources of authority and their conversion into power and influence. We shall demonstrate the gains in distinguishing conceptually authority, power, and influence. While formal organization structure distributes authority within the social space of positions, job content, and areas of responsibility over performance, authority remains static until individuals psychologically infuse it with energy, meaning, and value. This process of converting authority into power involves the relationship between the structure and the individuals who populate it. Conceptually, it shifts the focus of attention from the external structure to the internal work within the individual through which job definitions and areas of authority and responsibility become converted into intentions to act.[§]

Behavior itself, or putting intentions into action, is the process of influence. Here, the interest shifts again from what goes on inside the individual to interactions in which one person attempts to alter the thinking and behavior of another.

The research problem in this investigation begins with change in the formal organization structure. The initial questions are these:

(1) Does a change in structure in the direction of distributing authority downward in the organization actually result in its conversion into power among individuals at lower levels?

(2) To what extent do shifts in authority and its conversion into power held by individuals occupying positions become manifested and felt as influence in the working relationships among people?

(3) To what extent, if at all, does the downward shift in authority increase motivation to work, productivity, and job satisfaction? [§§]

Since the measurement aimed at answers to these questions involves responses at two points in time from individuals who occupy different positions in the organization, the data are comparative and utilize ordinal rather than absolute

---

[§] DALTON-BARNES comment: We differ conceptually on the power authority issue. In essence we view authority as being one (legitimated and circumscribed) form of power. According to this view, power is not derived from an organization's "external structure" or from an individual's "internal work," but rather from the nature of the power-dependency relationship. (See Chapter VII for a fuller explanation of this view.)

[§§] DALTON-BARNES comment: See Chapter VII for additional questions raised by Professors Dalton and Barnes.

scales. This fact about the measurement methods used in this study means that the analysis and interpretation of trends are subject to probabilistic judgments. There are no "all-or-nothing" answers available for the research questions. But the fact that the data produce trends and require "teasing out" and interpretation of answers is not simply a result of measurement problems. Human actions seldom produce effects according to intentions. We therefore adopt the position of healthy skepticism in viewing research results and urge the reader to do the same. This attitude of skepticism will in the end result in a greater degree of understanding of what occurs when leaders alter the formal organization structure to affect performance.

In appraising the research results, Chapter V will examine outcomes from the standpoint of the theory of change. Chapter VI by Professor Zaleznik and Chapter VII by Professors Barnes and Dalton will conclude this research report with interpretations and inferences concerning the management of authority and power. Because the co-authors of this study utilize different ideas both in exploring and in interpreting human action in organizations, the presentation of two concluding chapters seemed appropriate.

CHAPTER II

Case History

THE NAMPA Development Center is an organizational unit within the Westwood Division of the Norfleet Company, a large U.S. corporation. Norfleet can best be described as a "technology based" organization; its products, its manufacturing processes, and even the very industries in which it operates are products of modern technological invention. Norfleet was one of the original firms in the industry, and Norfleet's management has been justifiably proud of the company's successful record of technical innovation. Company officers frequently speak of Norfleet's "heritage of scientific and technical leadership" in their public statements and assert that this pride in past achievement is matched by a determination to continue a major emphasis on research and development.

These public statements particularly stress the company's dependence on the productive effort of its scientists and engineers. The annual report to stockholders each year contains a statement assuring the stockholders that the management recognizes that "the company's future is based in large measure on the abilities and initiative of its many hundreds of graduate scientists and technically trained people." In a recent speech to a meeting of stockbrokers, the president of Norfleet reaffirmed management's intention to "capitalize on the abilities of the company's scientists and technicians as the means of insuring an accelerated future growth." Recruitment brochures describe the company's efforts to "provide the best possible environment for technically trained people."

THE NAMPA DEVELOPMENT CENTER

During the period following World War II, the Westwood Division was created by Norfleet's management to exploit what was then a new area of technology which had grown from basic research discoveries at Norfleet's centralized research laboratories. The Westwood Division found a ready market for its products and soon became one of the company's most profitable divisions. In these early years the Division grew rapidly, building new facilities and hiring new people.

Creation of the Center

The Westwood Division soon established its own separate facilities for development work which came to be known as the Nampa Development Center. This Center was to act primarily as a bridge between Norfleet's central research laboratories and Westwood's production plants and marketing departments. The men at the Center were to develop into commercially producible products the scientific discoveries and technical innovations related to the Division's product family which resulted from the company's research activities. The first step in this process was the exploration of methods to produce the new product in large quantities. This often required fundamental changes in the basic product design. If, in fact, it was determined that the product could be produced in quantity, economic studies were then to be made to determine whether the product could be produced and sold profitably. If the product appeared promising, large-scale production problems would be worked out, production techniques developed, and equipment designed for a new or existing production plant.

In addition, the Center had two other major tasks: to improve existing products; and to help customers utilize existing products in new ways.

Early History of the Center

During the first few years of Nampa's history, most of the effort was devoted to exploiting the basic discovery which had launched the Westwood Division. The Center rapidly developed modifications of the original product and discovered a number of new commercial applications, as well as cheaper methods of production. After a few years, however, the rate of innovation began to decline. Much of the work at the Center in this product area went into modifying existing products to meet customer demands.

Development effort was then increasingly devoted to a new potential product called Filtron which, it was hoped, would lead the company into an entirely new industry. More and more time and energy were devoted to the Filtron Project until a sizable portion of the men at the Center were working on it alone. When it neared completion, however, and processes for manufacturing the new product were almost worked out, Norfleet's management decided neither to market nor to manufacture the Filtron units. This decision came as a sharp disappointment to the men who had been working on the Filtron Project, as well as to others at the Center. Many of the men who worked on the project had anticipated that as Filtron came to be an important product for the company, their own personal careers would be closely tied to its growth and to the related products which would follow. Even those who had not foreseen their own personal careers related directly to Filtron had hoped that the Filtron unit and its related products would bring another period of growth as in the early years at the Center.

During the same period that work on the Filtron Project was being discontinued and the men assigned to other projects, new price cuts were announced for the Division's major existing product. The company's early technological breakthrough, resulting in a strong patent and market position, had initially assured the Westwood Division of a high profit margin on this product. Other companies, however, had now entered the market and competition was driving prices down, sharply narrowing profits.

The men at the Center frequently complained that the Division was not experiencing the growth they had anticipated when they came to work for Westwood. They were further concerned because of the relative homogeneity in the ages of the managers and scientists at the Center. Both the technology underlying most of their work and the Nampa Center itself had been in existence less than 20 years. Those men who had begun the early work at the Center and who now held most of the top management positions were only a few years older than most of the men under them. The age span among the managers and scientists ranged only from the early twenties to the early forties. Management positions had opened up rapidly in the early years at the Center; now openings were coming slowly.

Some men were also disturbed by what they saw as a disappointing relationship between competence and results. Even though they saw themselves as more competent now at handling difficult technical problems than during their early years, this was not being translated into new products, greater sales, and company growth. One of the Group Leaders expressed this feeling as follows:

> What's wrong with us? We have plenty of good capable people around here. We can lick almost any technical problem we tackle, but it doesn't seem to do any good. We need to know what we should be working on. Better still, what should we stop working on? We need to know what would be most likely to produce the biggest profits for the company and help it grow again. Maybe we need to learn how to work with each other, I don't know.

Succession of a New Director

Early in 1960 a new man, Dr. West, was placed at the

head of the Center. Although new to this position, he was not new to the Center itself. He had worked at Nampa continuously in various capacities since shortly after its establishment, and prior to his promotion had been in charge of a large part of the Center's scientific and technical activities. The new director had both a strong academic background and a reputation for personal technical accomplishment. He was the only person in senior management ranks at the Center with a Ph.D. and during his early years at the Center, when his administrative duties were more limited, his own technical efforts had resulted in a substantial number of patents for the company.

The new Director made several changes in the senior management structure when he was first placed in charge of the Center. His predecessor had used the title of Plant Manager, and the organization structure had followed the pattern of the Division's production plants. The Plant Engineer, the Production Manager (in charge of pilot plant operations), the Personnel Manager, the Plant Accountant, and the Manager of Technical Services (Dr. West) had all reported directly to the Plant Manager. [See Figure 2]

FIGURE 2

PARTIAL ORGANIZATION CHART BEFORE THE NEW
DIRECTOR'S PROMOTION

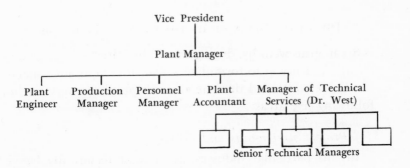

When the Plant Manager left the Development Center, and Dr. West was appointed to replace him, West changed the title of Plant Manager to Director of Development. He also decided to have a different group of persons reporting to him than had reported to his predecessor. A new position was created, entitled Manager of Administrative Services, to whom the Plant Engineer, the Production Manager, the Personnel Manager, and the Plant Accountant reported. He in turn reported to the Director. The Senior Technical Managers, who had reported directly to Dr. West as Manager of Technical Services, continued to report to him as Director. [See Figure 3]

FIGURE 3

PARTIAL ORGANIZATION CHART AFTER THE NEW
DIRECTOR'S PROMOTION

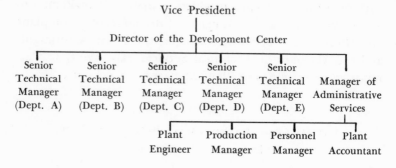

DIRECTOR'S DIAGNOSIS OF THE CENTER'S PROBLEMS

Six months went by, during which the Director studied the Center and began to formulate a plan for improving operations. He concluded that the Center's problems were in the following five areas:

(1) *Project stretch-outs and delays*

In this particular industry, as in most technically based

industries, the speed at which a new product could be developed and placed on the market had become an increasingly critical element in its profitability. Usually several companies worked on a similar product and a few months' lead often turned out to be the decisive competitive advantage. The new Director believed that several products had taken longer than necessary to reach the market. Delays had arisen in transferring products and information from research to development and from there to production and sales. Stretched-out completion dates had resulted in discouragement and complacency. Moreover, the need for profitable new products had been accentuated by the decreased profitability of the Division's major product and the discontinuance of the Filtron Project.

(2) *Inefficient use of technical abilities*

He was further concerned about inefficiencies in the utilization of the Center's technical skills. When a technical problem arose within one group, oftentimes no one within that group had the special background experience or skill to approach the problem effectively. And frequently, although someone else in the Center might already have acquired the specialized skills or knowledge needed, no one contacted him. In consequence, the group did a poor job or waited while someone in the group acquired the knowledge or skill to handle the problem. The Director believed that the Center had grown too rigid to allow the free flow of ideas, knowledge, and skills to focus on problems when they arose.

The management had hoped to obtain this free flow by establishing a staff specialist group during the previous year. They had placed in this group a number of the senior scientists with expertise in specialized areas of measurement, processes, and instrumentation. However, the staff specialist group had found it difficult to persuade men in the product development department to use them, despite management's repeated encouragement to do so. Management had even assigned certain specialists to work with groups encountering difficulties, but the staff specialists found it difficult to gain acceptance and exert influence. Two of the specialists commented on this problem:

> Our number-one problem is trying to work with other people on their problems without raising antagonisms. They seem to get the idea that we are trying to replace them. They give us little isolated parts of the problem to work on. Actually that places a serious limitation on us. The formulation of the problem and the research design are often the very areas where we can help most effectively. Sometimes they have problems that they don't know what to do with. Yet they are still reluctant to let anyone else know about them.

*   *   *   *   *

> All that we in the staff specialist group want is (a) to be helpful, and (b) get at least a minimum feeling of being a part of things. In some parts of the Center this works out fine. I go over there and I feel a part of things. They talk over the problem with me. Their problems are mine. I feel a responsibility to help solve them. In other parts I feel like I am going to be kicked out.

(3) *Cumbersome organization structure*

Here the Director's concerns were varied. He felt that the Center had grown "top heavy" — that there were too many levels of administration. Junior Managers (Group Leaders) were not being given overall responsibility for the accomplishment of their work. The Center no longer seemed to be the training ground for future managers that it had been during its early days. Moreover, responsibility for the successful completion of any one project was diffused among managers, supervisors, and group leaders. The Director wanted to move responsibility downward, allowing first level administration to play a more central role in the work of the Center:

> I would like to give our work groups specific tasks with the leader of the project having the responsibility and the authority necessary to get that task done in the shortest time possible. This Project Leader would still report directly to a Technical Manager, but I don't want that manager spending a lot of time directing details. Instead, I want to make it clear that this Project Leader is the person who will be responsible for getting this job done. I want him to have a chance to run exposed and show what he can do. I want to pinpoint responsibility for accomplishing a task.

He also hoped to engender in the Project Leaders a resistance to undue outside pressure.

> I would like to develop in the Project Leaders the feeling of autonomy and responsibility to the point where they will impose their opinion on outside groups — where they will be willing to stand up to any force, external to the group itself, which is trying to direct their activities. The men actually performing the work are in the best position to make the decisions about the technical work. If senior management or sales try to hurry them when it is impractical, I want them to stand up and say so. Too many times I find people doing what I say, even when they disagree silently. They don't speak up. The people who work closest to me have learned to speak up but sometimes the younger men don't. This can get us into trouble.

(4) *Insufficient long-range technical planning*

The Director felt strongly that not enough people were thinking about the technical needs of the Division five years hence. Too little attention was being given to a broad examination of the direction of their efforts. Someone, he said, should be asking whether their present efforts made sense in the light of recent and projected trends in their industry and in society in general. This lack of long-range planning, he said, resulted in spending too much development effort on minor modifications and improvements on existing products. In the absence of longer-term objectives, frequent requests from sales for product modifications swallowed up too much of the development capacity.

(5) *Morale problems*

Finally, morale was a concern. The Director wanted the men to feel a greater sense of identification with their projects and with the success of the company. He hoped to promote a stronger sense of pride in accomplishment throughout the Center, and particularly among the staff specialists, whose only assignment was to provide advice and services for other groups on their projects.

A PLAN FOR REORGANIZING SOME DEPARTMENTS

The Director had formulated a plan for reorganizing parts of the Center which he felt would simultaneously help correct several of the problems listed. The plan was designed to affect directly only half the departments, those which were already most directly involved in the development of new products. The other departments were to remain relatively unaffected.

The anticipated changes in these experimental departments can be placed under four headings:

(1) The organization structure in these departments was to be "flattened" through the elimination of one level of senior management.

(2) Project Groups were to be used as the central unit of organization, with a Junior Manager (the Project Leader) having primary responsibility for completion of the assignment given his group.

(3) Interfunctional committees at the Junior Manager level between Research, Development, and Sales were to be formed. These committees would be responsible for the accelerated development of specific new products.

(4) The Senior Technical Managers in these departments were to divorce themselves from much of the daily administration of the groups in their departments and spend half their time on long-range technical planning.

Eliminating the Supervisors in the Experimental Departments

Within each of the departments the administrative structure had previously consisted of three levels of supervision: two levels of senior management, the Senior Technical Managers and the Supervisors, and one level of junior management, the Group Leaders. Some Group Leaders had reported directly to a Senior Technical Manager, others had worked under Supervisors who themselves reported to a Technical Manager. [See Figure 4]

FIGURE 4

PRIOR DEPARTMENTAL ORGANIZATION STRUCTURE

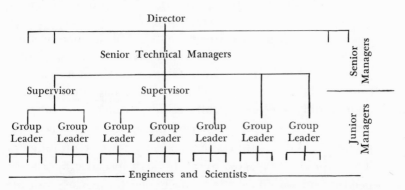

The Director proposed to eliminate the Supervisor level in the experimental departments. Thus all the men in those departments who headed up a group of engineers or scientists would now report directly to a Senior Technical Manager. Some of the Supervisors whose jobs were thus eliminated were to be asked to head up single groups themselves, taking Junior Manager positions. Others were asked to assume staff positions. The Director planned to give these former Supervisors some of the most important problems in the Center to work on, and in doing so expressed the hope that he could downgrade the importance of position-level at the Center.

> What I would like to create around here is a problem orientation. I would like to have people feel that their status comes from the difficulty and importance of the problems to which they are assigned rather than from the number of levels between them and the Vice President. Their power should come from what they know, not how many people report to them.

The Junior Managers in the Experimental Departments

The key men in the new structure were to be the Junior Managers, the leaders of the Project Groups. Personnel within the groups were not to be substantially different in make-up from the existing groups. Most Junior Managers would be supervising the same men as before. The change was in the scope and nature of the duties of the men heading up these groups. Each group would have a specific objective. Some would be working on the improvement of an existing product; others would be developing a new product; but each would have measurable technical objectives and time goals. The Junior Managers would plan their own technical programs, budgets, timetables, and manpower requirements. They would be expected to call for staff specialist help when needed and would be the contact men for persons outside the Center interested in their work. Figure 5 represents the anticipated departmental structure.

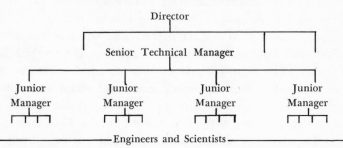

FIGURE 5

NEW ORGANIZATION STRUCTURE IN THE
EXPERIMENTAL DEPARTMENTS

The CAPS Committees

A further part of the plan was to assign the Junior Managers in the experimental departments to interdivisional committees. One of the Director's aims was to make each Junior Manager the chief point of contact for persons outside the Center concerned with his project. In the past, men from outside the Center had exerted every effort to contact a Senior Manager rather than deal with a lower status Junior Manager.

This proposal meshed with the aim of a new Vice President of Research and Development for the Norfleet Company. The new Vice President sought some better way of coordinating work in the Company's central research laboratories with the development work in each of the divisions. Out of exploratory talks came a proposal to set up joint committees with members from the central research laboratories, the division sales staff, and the Development Center. This came to be known as the "Coordinated Action Program," or the CAPS committees. The stated purpose of these committees was to coordinate the efforts of research development and sales toward the rapid achievement of specific objectives resulting in either a profitable new product or a major improvement in an existing product. The major questions at the Center were, "What should be worked on?" "How much time and effort should be applied to the development of a potential new product?" "How much of the Center's efforts should be devoted to the improvement of a certain existing product?" In the past, these questions had been handled in part by the Senior Technical Managers in response to customer needs reported by Sales and new ideas coming from the research laboratories. The Senior Managers headed up departments organized around major product areas, and when a customer problem arose which existing products could not solve competitively, the sales people first went to the Customer Services Department. If the problem could not be solved by minor product modification, the sales people then approached a Senior Technical Manager, asking him to put a man on it. Also, when ideas for new products came from the Research Laboratories, the Senior Technical Manager from the most closely related product area usually assigned men to work on its development.

Dr. West felt that the result of this style of operation had been to diffuse development efforts. People at the Center were working on too many things and applying too little effort to the most promising new products. Through the assignments to the new CAPS groups, he hoped to focus efforts on developing a small number of promising new products or major improvements in existing products.

Although such a program would divert effort from exploratory research activities, the Vice President and the Director of the Research Laboratories were willing to try out the idea. Both expressed the hope that the committees would provide a model for relations between the Research Laboratories and the Development Centers in other divisions of the company. The Vice President of Sales in the Westwood Division similarly agreed to assign men from Sales to each of the committees.

Senior Managers Assigned to Long-Range Planning

The final aspect of the Director's plan was his assignment of Senior Managers in the experimental departments to long-range planning. No one else, he said, was as well qualified to do this job. The expanded duties of the Junior Managers would thus relieve the Senior Managers in the experimental departments of daily administrative responsibilities, freeing them to spend half their time on longer-range planning. He proposed to have them "sit down and do some serious thinking about what we should be doing here technically, three, four, five years from now." He intended that these Senior Managers spend no more than half their time managing their departments. They would not be appointed to or even attend any of the interdivisional CAPS committees. Moreover, they were to refer anyone seeking information about one of their groups to the Project Leader.

INITIATING CHANGES WITHIN THE CENTER

During the early months following his appointment, the Director had outlined problems, solicited ideas, and discussed possible remedies at several meetings, including one with all the managers and scientists in the Center. These meetings had been largely exploratory, and no definite organizational changes had been initiated or even proposed. When he had formulated a general program which he felt would address the problems of the Center, the Director began a second series of meetings to propose and initiate the changes he sought.

Presenting the Plan to the Senior Managers

First he held a series of special meetings with the Senior Managers (often after hours) to discuss the changes, explain his aims, and plan for an implementation of his program in the experimental departments. The Senior Managers raised many questions about the workability and the implementation of the plan. Afterward the Director reported that the Senior Managers were the most severe critics of the plan.

> The major resistance I have gotten so far has come from the Senior Managers. I guess I am asking for a bigger change for them than from anyone else. In a couple of the departments there are now practically no decisions made without the Senior Managers being in on them. They are as busy as they can be, coordinating and supervising the groups under them. They don't really believe that these Project Leaders can do all the things they will be asked to do without a great deal of help. They claim that the new program will take more of the managers' time rather than less. Actually I think the prospect of having all this day-to-day work taken away from them is disturbing.

Several men at the Center who heard of the proposals thought that the Senior Managers in the experimental departments were actually being "moved aside" so that the men under them could take the reins. They predicted that the Senior Managers would lose status by this move:

> I don't see how a guy can be a manager of a department without getting involved in administrative problems. Dick West says he wants the Senior Managers to stay out of these problems and just be managers of technical affairs. But I say a manager should manage people, money, and supplies. He can't do that by managing technical problems. If a guy is going to be a manager, he should manage.

The Senior Managers reported in interviews that they were in complete agreement with a number of the plan's features. They agreed, first, that the Supervisor level in the management structure was probably unnecessary, and second, that it was good to give the younger men, who had previously had little opportunity, a chance to show what they could do. However, they questioned whether the Director was moving too fast, too far, and warned that with the Junior Managers competing for equipment and services, demands on the Senior Managers' time would actually be increased. They foresaw little released time for long-range planning and predicted real difficulties in convincing outsiders to contact the Junior Managers rather than themselves. People outside the division, they said, always tried to contact someone on the Senior Manager level or above. The Senior Managers had spent many years building a wide and complex set of relationships with those outside the Center who were concerned with their work, and they thought this would not easily change. They also questioned whether the Junior Managers could handle all the outside contacting and still adequately manage project work in their groups.

The Director discussed each of these points with the Senior Managers, made minor modifications, but maintained his plan's essential structure, insisting that they would be able to work out these problems.

Announcing the Change to the Project Leaders

When the time finally arrived to announce the program to the Project Leaders, the Senior Managers reported that they were still not in complete agreement but were willing to go along and try it out. They worked diligently to help the Director plan how the program would be presented to the Junior Managers who would act as the Project Leaders.

All the Junior Managers in the experimental departments, as well as their Senior Managers, were called together. The Director outlined the changes being made and stressed the responsibilities of the Project Leaders. Each Junior Manager in charge of a project would be expected to:

(1) Plan the technical work for his project.
(2) Set up a timetable for the completion of various phases of the project.
(3) Plan the budget for the program.

(4) Plan the manpower requirements for meeting his objectives.

(5) Seek help when needed from the various specialists at the Development Center.

(6) Monitor the progress of his project and recommend changes in the budget, manpower, or timetable when the project slips behind schedule.

(7) Provide necessary training for group personnel, coordinate their activities, and evaluate their performance. Participate with manager in recommendations for promotions and salary increases.

(8) Maintain contact with those persons outside the Center concerned with the project (i.e., representatives from Research, Sales, and Production).

The Director told the men that he expected the company to benefit greatly from the changes, but also stressed the expected benefits for them, listing (1) the new responsibilities being given them which were presently handled by Senior Managers; (2) the opportunity to demonstrate their ability to handle these responsibilities; (3) the opportunity to improve their management ability by actual practice; and (4) the chance for them to apply their full effort to a program of great importance where the results could be readily seen by company management.

He also described the new planning responsibilities of the Senior Managers and pictured the more restricted role he expected them to play in their departments.

He pointed out to the Junior Managers that they were going to need all the help they could get from other sources, and urged them to make full use of the staff specialists to help them solve their problems. They themselves would have to pass down some of their own responsibilities to the men under them if they hoped to make rapid progress.

It was his aim that everyone involved in the change would have a greater opportunity to exert an influence and an expanded role in the success of the organization. Not only were the Junior Managers being given expanded responsibilities, but their need for help and advice would also require the members of their groups and the staff specialists to share in this responsibility. The Senior Managers, he said, could have the greatest potential impact of all, not only on the Center but on the future direction of the Division.

The presentation ended with the announcement that each Junior Manager was to begin immediately to prepare a budget to be ready in three weeks for his project for the coming year. Senior Managers previously had handled budget projections.

The predominant response was favorable but reserved. The following comments from two of the Junior Manager-Project Leaders were typical:

> I think this program is going to have a positive effect on our work. All the Project Leaders are going to try harder to prove themselves. My Supervisor had had too much to handle effectively before. I used to have to wait for him to make decisions. Now I will be able to make them myself.

*   *   *   *   *

> I think this will work if it receives the sustaining force from Dr. West on down. If he means what he says — that the Project Leaders are really in charge of the projects — then I am going to be glad to take it on and try to make it work.

The assignment to prepare budget projections and requests seemed particularly significant to one Project Leader:

> I was surprised that things were made as specific as they were. I particularly didn't expect to make budget projections so soon. I think I am beginning to understand what Dr. West is doing.

Some Junior Managers felt confused:

> I don't know how to take this new assignment. It is not a

promotion. There is no change in my classification and no salary increase.

Others wondered if the Senior Managers would really let go:

Some of the Senior Managers like to keep their finger on things. I know the Senior Manager in this department will find it very hard to let much control go out of his hands.

Others, who apparently felt more dependent on the Senior Managers, were concerned that the manager would be too far removed. One Project Leader said he hoped the new approach would not prevent his Senior Manager from making suggestions, as he did not want to lose the ideas and experience of his superior. Another wondered whether his boss would be around enough to appraise his work.

I like someone above to know what I am doing — to recognize a good job.

All the Project Leaders recognized that their new assignment would increase their work load. Some proposed to handle this by passing more of the responsibility and decision making down to their own subordinates, but for some, this posed a serious dilemma:

To make this program succeed, we are going to have to push responsibility down to our men. This is where we get into a problem. I don't think I should push technical decisions down. That means I will just have to absorb more work. It will mean that I will have to spend *more* time right there with them at the bench making sure they are at maximum efficiency.

Announcement to the Senior and Junior Scientists

Most of the nonsupervisory scientists involved were told of the changes by their Group Leaders. A few were assigned to work under a new group head but most continued under their present chief. Several weeks after the announcement some had heard nothing about a change. Among the scientists who had been told of the change, there was general agreement that removing one level in the management structure would be useful. Some men reported having received orders from both their Group Leader and their Supervisor, and it had been difficult at times to move their ideas and recommendations up through so many levels of administration. Beyond this, the reaction tended to be neutral and somewhat skeptical that any change in actual behavior would result.

> I would say I am numb to the whole idea. I find it a little difficult to believe it will work the way Dr. West says it will. I would like to see it work, but I don't think it will. Most of us were at the meeting when Dr. West first presented the Project Group idea to the scientists. I would characterize the feelings of the people there as one of general skepticism. I think that people are just skeptical about the Project Group idea rather than being definitely against it. I think that with the Project Groups, results won't be very much different from what they have been before. Why make such a big change if it isn't going to help any?

*   *   *   *   *

> I feel generally neutral about the change, although it does have some possibilities.

ESTABLISHING THE CAPS COMMITTEES

Budget preparation was only the first of the new assignments for the Project Leaders. Their new role began to sharpen even further as the divisional Coordinating Action Program (CAPS) committees were set up jointly by Dr. West, the Director of the Research Laboratories, and the Vice President of Sales in the Westwood Division. Each CAPS committee was composed of at least three men: (1) a

Group Leader or Supervisor from the Research Laboratories; (2) a Project Leader from the Development Center; and (3) a Product Manager from the divisional sales office. The Project Leader from the Development Center would direct the efforts of his group in carrying out the development portion of the tasks assigned his CAPS committee. He was assigned to coordinate closely the efforts of his group with the work being done on the assigned task in other parts of the company.

When the CAPS committees were set up, a Senior Scientist from one of the staff support groups whose specialty was particularly needed was assigned to work with each Project Group working with a CAPS committee. This specialist was not to be a member of the group and would not report to the Junior Manager who acted as Project Leader. Instead, he was assigned as an advisor to provide special services and to act as a liaison man with other staff specialists. The Project Leader could take members of his group or the assigned Senior Scientist with him to CAPS committee meetings when he chose to do so.

Technical Objectives and Time Goals

To establish objectives (in terms of product characteristics) for the CAPS committees, the Director met with the management from Research Laboratories and from Divisional Sales, as well as with his own Senior Managers, to determine which new product ideas and which major product modifications appeared to hold the greatest potential. The number was narrowed down from 50 items to 19, with a few groups working on two or three modifications.

Each committee had product specifications and a specific target date for putting its product into production. Time goals were heavily stressed. Each committee was to turn in a projected schedule broken down by weeks. If the committee members concluded that the specifications were not

achievable or the target date unrealistic, they were responsible for defending this conclusion to the Directors.

Decision Making in the Committee

The committees, "working as a unit," were to make the
decisions necessary to plan the work, project joint budgets,
direct the experiments, design the equipment, and keep
others informed of their progress. The Senior Managers, who
were not members of these committees, would therefore not
be present while the decisions were made. A written directive
sent to persons both inside and outside the Center made
explicit that it was the CAPS committee members who were
to hold the responsibility for the direction of work. The
directive included the following statement:

> Multiple responsibility for the direction of these Project
> Committees has been set up. Individuals assigned by Re-
> search, Development, and Sales have been given the respon-
> sibility by their respective departments to coordinate and
> direct the CAPS committee program.

No chairmen were assigned. Each committee was to choose
its own chairman or rotate the chairman's responsibility.
Chairmen were to call and conduct meetings but were given
no directive authority over other members. Influence in
the meetings was to be exerted through ideas, information,
and persuasion.

Even the avenue of "bucking up a decision" to a common
superior was not readily available to the members of these
committees. The Research Laboratories were not a part of
the Westwood Division; hence the members of the CAPS
committees shared no common superior below the corporate
vice president level. Even the Directors of the Research Laboratories and the Development Center shared no common
immediate superior.

Reporting Procedures

Finally, each committee was required to make an oral progress report every three weeks to a review board at the Development Center composed of the Vice President of Development in the Westwood Division, the Director of the Research Laboratories, and the Director of the Development Center. The report was to be made by the current chairman of each committee. Whenever a Project Leader from the Center reported to the board, his Senior Manager was to accompany him. If the committee was behind schedule, the members were expected to come in with a recommendation for increased manpower or budget to bring themselves back up to schedule or else to recommend a revised schedule.

POTENTIAL PROBLEMS

Men at the Center were divided in their predictions concerning the effects of the Director's proposals. Some felt that the changes could bring about a substantial alteration in the operations of the product development departments. Others predicted that actual changes would be negligible, that everyone would carry out his work and his relations with others much as before. Nearly everyone interviewed, however, agreed that the Director's proposal would encounter several major difficulties:

(1) It would be difficult for the Senior Managers in the experimental departments to relinquish control and decision making to the Junior Managers now acting as Project Leaders. The Senior Managers still felt personal responsibility for the progress of the work in their departments. Moreover, the Senior Managers, and the Project Leaders had established relationships in which more direction from the superior was expected than was now proposed. Finally, the Senior Managers were being

asked to move from familiar to unfamiliar activities, from immediate to future problems and from work which produces relatively concrete and tangible output toward work where the output is intangible.

(2) It would be difficult to establish the Project Leaders as the primary contact men with outsiders. Sales managers, research personnel, and others would continue to press for information and decisions from the Senior Managers as they had in the past.

(3) Previously, the product development groups had not made effective use of the staff specialists. It was still unclear how this problem would be affected by the changes made.

(4) No new sense of urgency, or enthusiasm, was evident among the Junior Scientists in the project groups.

The Director stated that he was aware of these problems. They had been anticipated in making his proposal and, with effort, each could be overcome.

SUMMARY

Soon after a new Director had been appointed at the Nampa Center, development work was discontinued on a major project and prices began to fall on the Division's major existing product. The Director, already concerned about the effectiveness of the Center's efforts, proposed a series of changes designed to accelerate the development of new products and involve the men more deeply in their work.

One level of supervision was eliminated; Senior Managers were assigned half-time to planning activities, and Junior Managers (Project Leaders) were assigned decision-making functions performed previously by Senior Managers. Interdivisional (CAPS) coordinating committees were set up with heads of the Development Center, the Research Center, and the Marketing Department establishing specific objectives and completion dates. Junior Managers represented the Development Center on the CAPS committees, coordinating the efforts of their groups with groups in Research and Sales. A Senior Scientist from the staff specialist group was assigned to work with each product development group.

These were the events, described in terms used by the participants, and the organizational variables which were being explicitly altered to achieve stated aims. These events, however, markedly affected other variables in the organization as well, raising for consideration prior solutions to the problem of the distribution of authority, power, and influence. To appreciate this impact, we need to re-examine the events already discussed, using a new set of terms and a different conceptual framework This will be the task of Chapter III.

CHAPTER III

Authority, Power, and Influence

THE WORD "authority," while one of the most frequently used terms in managment theory, is subject to many interpretations. Appendix B presents a review of the pertinent issues in the theory of authority and organizational change.

Study of Appendix B will demonstrate that a good part of the ambiguity in authority as a concept and even in its practical extensions stems from the following sources:

1. The prevalence in using authority interchangeably as a structural and dynamic variable. As a structural variable the concept of authority yields certain clarifications about different *types* of authority inherent in the organization and related to the wider social organization. As a dynamic variable the term authority often refers to the means by which changes in attitudes and behavior occur.

2. The tendency to ignore the fact that the uses of authority involve individual thought and action. The theory of authority, therefore, if treated solely as a sociological issue, will overlook the psychological aspects of individual action and reaction to organization structure.

3. The absence of clarity in considering authority in both its quantitative and its qualitative aspects. There is an amount of authority subject to distribution in an organization, but there are also different *types* of authority imbedded in the structure.§ Alteration in the authority structure may

---

§ DALTON-BARNES COMMENT: To us, the assumption of a fixed quantity of authority in an organization, capable of distribution but not expansion or contraction, is open to serious question. This assumption seems most questionable when authority is defined broadly, as it is here, to include

change either or both the quantitative distribution and the type of authority which has primacy in the minds of members of the organization.

4. The readiness to accept implicit definitions of rationality in organizational actions while overlooking the idea that rationality and irrationality are not paired opposites but rather are subject to interpretation at the levels of the organization, the group, and the individual. The question of rationality in authority is complicated by the fact that the attempt to change the organization structure involves the uses of authority identified with the office and person of the chief executive. The direction of change may therefore evoke conflicts of interest which involve equally rational but opposing ends and control of means.

5. The displacement of normative concerns into the language of investigation and inquiry. Many writers and practitioners are really interested in changing organization or management as their first order of business. Currently, the direction of change is toward shifting authority from the top to the bottom of the organization. While this concern for equalizing authority may be a good thing, the problem for investigators is to remain objectively neutral on types of changes and their outcomes.

This chapter will consider these five problems in the theory of authority in an effort to sort out the many dimensions to authority in its theoretical and applied aspects. The Nampa case history presented in Chapter II lends itself to interpretation in the light of the clarifications developed in this chapter.

---

knowledge-based as well as position-based authority. As individual members develop recognized expertise, knowledged-based authority seems clearly expansible, and not necessarily at the expense of positional authority. But even when the focus is restricted to positional authority, the fixed-sum assumption is questionable. As an organization moves toward clearer specifications and greater acceptance of differentiated roles, it is not only possible but probable that the total amount of authority will expand.

AUTHORITY AND INFLUENCE §

A widely accepted definition of authority in classical sociological theory asserts that authority exists only when compliance with directives occurs. Voluntary compliance depends on the perception by subordinates that those who issue directives are acting within their rights — that the initiation of action is legitimate. It is not simply idiosyncratic judgments about legitimacy, but instead, the perception that a person has the right to initiate actions by others has to be widely held within the context of a group.[1] Authority therefore is the commonly accepted right to direct and alter behavior held as a general value judgment in the minds of those who initiate and act upon directives. The term directive does not limit this definition of authority; it can refer to verbal or written means of expressing direction for other people's behavior.

Influence is a term with wider and broader connotations than authority. Any successful direction or alteration in behavior represents influence whether it is seen as legitimate or in violation of accepted values and quite apart from the means used to alter behavior. In this sense, all authority is subsumed under the term influence, but there are certain types of influence, mainly coercive, which are not considered authority as it was defined earlier.

Among the many problems which arise in these definitions, two demand attention in relation to the problem of formal organization structure: (1) what attributes of authority are inherent and specific to formal organization structure; (2) are there differences between authority and influence more

---

[1] Reference footnotes will be found at the end of this book beginning on page 213.

---

§ DALTON-BARNES COMMENT: A different formulation of the power, authority, influence relationship is described in Chapter VII.

significant for the analysis of organization structure than simply the question of legitimacy of directives.

A formal organization structure is an autonomous symbol of relationships which can be described apart from value orientations of individuals and groups. It is an imperative and expresses what should exist in the relationships among members. The formal structure therefore becomes an input designed to channel the behavior of people who elect to work in an organization. The public presentation of the structure is an attempt at influence in that it prescribes how people should behave in relation to the communications which emanate from particular positions described in the structure.

The concept of authority in formal organization structure is more specifically the intended direction and content of influence. Whether attempts to influence are completely successful does not diminish the existence or significance of the formal organization structure and its prescribed patterns of influence. The fact that most individuals may not follow these prescribed patterns completely and instead respond to influence not encompassed in the structure also does not diminish the significance of the formal organization as an input affecting thought and action.

From the standpoint of formal organization structure, it seems more appropriate to consider authority as the prescribed expectations that one individual should exert control and direction over other individuals within defined areas of competence. Authority is therefore a structural variable, initially external to individuals who populate organizations. The use of authority to alter behavior is the process of influence which converts a latent attribute of the organization structure into a manifest demand from one person to others on expected action. What stands between authority as a structural variable and influence as an outcome of interpersonal events concerns the work which goes on within individuals in response to the authority in the structure, or its intended uses to affect behavior. We shall consider this issue of work within individuals when discussing power.

In considering authority as a structural variable which becomes active when men begin to communicate intentions and directions for others, it is immediately obvious that the structure of authority can take many forms and is subject to alteration. The obligations and right to create or change an authority structure are basic to the core authority relationship between the chief executive officer and his immediate superior. This relationship may be between a president and the board of directors, or, as in the Nampa case, between the head of an auxiliary organization and his immediate superior in the central organization. Organization charts do not arise full-blown out of corporate charters or tradition. They represent decisions on the part of the top officer to distribute authority according to a selected pattern.

The traditional concept of authority with its emphasis on voluntary compliance leaves a large gap between authority as a structural variable and influence as actual direction of behavior. This gap is not closed satisfactorily by noting that influence occurs in ways other than compliance to directives as, for example, in coercion and persuasion.

This traditional view both overstates the significance of compliance in organizations and understates involvement in activating authority in the formal structure. There is far less compliance, except for the trivial areas of work life, than is presumed in this earlier concept of authority. The involvement of individuals in giving meaning and value to the authority structure as manifested in persuasion, coercion, bargaining, and direct emotional appeals cannot be viewed as an extra-organizational phenomenon. To do so diminishes the importance of the formal organization structure which, as we have indicated, is a significant input in prescribing a pattern of authority relationships.

Turning now to the Nampa case study, the Director, acting within the right of his top position in the organization, promulgated a new normative structure of authority. His actions in establishing this new structure involved considerable discussion and persuasion to create acceptance and identification with the new plan. These efforts to influence members to accept the plan grew out of recognition that the Director's position alone could not activate the plan since the authority relations in the new structure embodied changes of major significance to the careers of many people. The plan increased the authority of Junior Managers and diminished the authority of mid-level supervisors by eliminating their positions. The new structure also created an ambiguous position for Senior Managers, since, while they continued to occupy the position and hold the title, their scope of activities was so different as to lead to the conclusion that their authority had been reduced.

In no sense could the Director's plan be considered trivial. Its potential impact on the range and scope of activities and consequently on the careers of individuals made the change a highly charged event. Whatever final results in the structure of authority and the process of influence, the changes initiated psychological work within the individuals to assess their position and response to the new organization chart. This silent work which ensues within individuals is the intervening variable between the input of structural change and the outcome of interaction, performance, and productivity. We shall use the term power as one dimension to this intervening variable and distinguish it from authority and influence.

POWER

The structure of authority represented in the formal organization plan defines the direction and content of attempts to influence behavior. For influence to occur, individuals involved in a set of relationships need to arrive at conceptions of authority intrinsic to their respective positions, their job descriptions, and their personality.

Power is the potential one individual has to guide, direct, control, or alter the behavior of others. Individuals in organizations differ in their power depending on how they bring together the authority stemming from their location in the formal organization structure, and made personal by an assessment of themselves and their goals in being a member of a particular organization.[2] An individual may have considerable authority as compared with other members of the organization, but he may have little desire to use this authority, or diffuse intentions, or an aversion to activity in favor of passivity. In such circumstances the individual has little power or, as defined above, a low potential to affect other people in their thoughts or actions. In the opposite case, where an individual is highly motivated to act and to influence others, but has little authority related to the formal organization, then his power may also be low.

Under certain circumstances, particularly in reform or revolutionary movements, individuals with forceful personalities achieve considerable influence apart from holding positions of authority in formal structures. The theory of charismatic leadership takes account of the impact of the emotional ties between leader and led usually in the form of the individual leader and the masses. But the concept of charisma also has application in formal organizations. Individuals who occupy positions with defined authority in the structure have a greater potential for attracting the emotional investments of subordinates. The degree to which these emotional bonds are developed defines the power one individual holds to exert influence over another. This power results from the acceptance of his authority by the office holder and the use of his personality in endowing authority with meaning for himself and other individuals within a context of objective goals, and means for achieving goals. There is no power to exert influence apart from some emotional elements in a relationship, but there is also usually little power apart from the consolidation within an individual of authority inherent in his position in a social structure.

Later in this chapter the discussion of sources of authority in the structure will clarify just what the individual may draw upon in developing power. But what needs emphasis at this point is that whatever the sources, the establishment of power occurs when individuals take within themselves or make internal what in the first instance is external and an attribute of the structure. The process of internalization and consolidation is a continuing function of individual decisions to participate in organizations. The power any person holds is therefore subject to constant accretions or diminutions. As other writers have shown,[3] the power an individual holds may be changed depending upon his success in influencing others. If he fails to influence, then his power is reduced. If he fails to try to influence when others expect him to, then his power will also decrease. Finally, if he succeeds in influencing others, but the direction proves wrong in the light of experience, then this situation will also result in the executive's loss of power.[§]

---

§ DALTON-BARNES COMMENT: Unquestionably, the desires, intentions, and style of an individual help determine the nature of the relationship he has with others in the organization. But to us, the terms power and authority are most fruitfully reserved for describing attributes of the *relationship* rather than of the *individual*. Authority, according to this view, is a legitimated and restricted form of power. (For a discussion of power examined from this viewpoint, see Chapter VII.)

In our view, power does *not* occur when individuals "take within themselves" what was external but occurs only when *another* party becomes dependent upon the first party. To assume that internal, intrapsychic work equals power is to assume that the Walter Mittys or Don Quixotes of the world hold power equal to presidents, kings, or dictators. Those who do only "psychological work within" risk delusions of grandeur unless other parties get involved in actual dependency relationships. The crux of power, then

These decreases or increases in power as a result of executive actions are not simply a function of changes in perceptions of the executive, but also the effects on the executive himself when he experiences successes and failures in influence. The attempts at influence involve individuals in representing and communicating to others the direction of influence, its intended results, and also the power they bring to the relationship.

The term power often connotes immoral or Machiavellian aspects of human relationships. Or, it connotes the use of aggression in one person dominating another. While these connotations are widely held, they obscure an idea which needs emphasis: that affecting outcomes in any sphere of human activity involves individuals in using themselves. These self assertions express power. Unless one visualizes passive individuals, the notion of power, the bases upon which it is established and how it is used, becomes an important variable in all human sciences and especially in the fields of organization and management.[4]

In the Nampa case study, the distribution of authority through change in formal organization structure initiated psychological work within individuals leading to new definitions of power relationships in the organization. By shifting authority among levels in the organization structure, individuals faced new opportunities and limitations in their capacity for, and modes of, influence.

The Director of the Center, for example, while the initiator of change, was also involved in redefining his power in the organization. At first glance it may appear as though he was relinquishing power through "flattening" the organization structure. Another interpretation of the effects of flattening leads to the conclusion that if anything his power increased through several effects. First, the new organization

is not what goes on within an individual, but what goes on between individuals.

structure created a stronger bond between the Director and Junior Managers while weakening their bond with Senior Managers. Not only was the Director responsible for enhancing the authority in the job of Junior Manager, but he also had more direct contact with them by appraising and guiding their work through the budget and evaluation meetings without the intermediate relationship with the Senior Managers.

Second, the CAPS committees gave the Director greater scope throughout the organization since his representatives, the Junior Managers, were in more frequent and direct communication with agents of the marketing, production, and research departments. In this sense, the Director both commanded and distributed more widely throughout the organization valuable resources such as projects, contact, and visibility in the organization.

The Junior Managers, as a result, had new options available to them in their technical work, and in their participation with superordinates, peers, and subordinates. Among these new options not the least significant was how they could marshal and in turn distribute resources to subordinates and Senior Scientists. The net effect was enhanced authority for Junior Managers and consequently new sources of power.[§]

In line with this interpretation the changes created problems for Senior Managers. The most reasonable conclusion is that the changes lessened their authority because the Senior Managers were stripped of resources which could be used to draw subordinates into a close working relationship with them. The new emphasis on long-range planning, while offered as a substitute for the loss of direct contact with subordinates, was at best an alternate way of building power in the organization, but one which involved considerable time to establish and to represent to others.

---

§ DALTON-BARNES COMMENT: But note that this also increased their dependency on others (notably on other members of the CAPS committees).

Just what bases the new organization structure offered individuals for establishing and consolidating power depended upon the shifts in authority envisioned within the new plan. These shifts involved quantitative and qualitative manipulations of authority.

These two aspects of the authority structure have general significance. Authority, while in the final analysis a quantitative variable, is also made up of elements closely related to job responsibilities and areas of competence.

QUANTITATIVE AND QUALITATIVE ASPECTS OF AUTHORITY

Historically, the concept of authority has been a center of controversy because of divergent views of organization.* One method of analysis distinguishes among types of authority in modern organizations, centering on the distinction between positional and professional authority.

Positional authority arises from the implicit or explicit agreement among members of an organization to designate the rights of individuals to direct the activities of others within prescribed limits. When a person joins an organization, he anticipates that he will receive direction from persons designated as superiors in the organizational hierarchy. It is a part of the employment contract. Partly as a means of supporting this authority, the holders of given positions are granted the right to dispense certain organizational rewards and punishments, such as dismissal, remuneration, and promotion.

Professional authority usually arises from the needs of formal organizations for application of specialized knowledge and expertise. The use of professional authority depends on the recognition that an individual possesses relevant expertise gained through education. Widely recognized symbols of professional training such as the Ph.D., M.D., or C.P.A.

---

* See Appendix B for a review of the concept of authority in the sociological literature.

provide the initial foundation for acceptance of authority derived from specialized knowledge. The symbols must be supported, however, by the demonstrated capacity of experts to use their knowledge effectively. The uses of expertise reward others in helping men solve problems. But the rewards are less direct as compared with the rewards surrounding positional authority. The potential punishment in professional authority is the capacity to withhold help and lessened ability to solve problems or to perform tasks effectively; the organizational rewards and sanctions of dismissal, promotion, and remuneration are thus affected, but only indirectly; the effect is one step removed.

The relation between positional and professional authority is increasingly a problem in modern organizations. The tasks performed by organizations are becoming much more complex technologically, and the men performing these tasks are more specialized in their training. As a consequence, supervisors are not able to match subordinates in the range of knowledge represented in their collective functions. When an individual needs help in solving a problem in his specialized function, his immediate supervisor may be ill-equipped to help, increasing the range of dependency relationships beyond the immediate work group. Contrary to the traditional expectation that those holding hierarchical authority are also the technical experts, the current situation in all organizations suggests a split between managerial and technical skills. This split does not imply that any one individual uses authority arising from only one source. The uses of different types of authority overlap in the activities of one individual. One man may simultaneously use authority in a group on the basis of his formal position in the organization, his high professional competence, and his well-developed interpersonal relations. Or he may depend on authority derived from different sources in different settings in the same organization. In one setting where he is working only with peers in the formal organization, his authority may rest primarily on his technical knowledge. In another setting, he may be working with subordinates where they respond to his suggestions almost solely in terms of his organizational position, giving little weight to his technical competence.

The individual's style of work and the way he develops power reflect the particular mode of synthesizing both professional and positional authority. The existence of both types does not obviate the need for individual synthesis. In addition, the particular synthesis is subject to alteration resulting from changes within the organization and within the individual.

One of the problems in the relationship between positional and professional authority concerns the element of primacy. The two sources of authority may be competitive, particularly as they exert a pull on the individual in the kind of power he establishes within his sphere of activity. While efforts to rationalize organizations lean heavily, as in the Nampa case, on the ascendancy of professional authority at the expense of positional authority, the tendency may exist over the long run for positional authority to resume a primacy position. As specialists gain promotions, for example, they move upward in the hierarchy and away from specific applications of knowledge and technique. This trend may be expressed as the movement from the specialist to the generalist position, or from staff to line work.

Whatever the genesis of competition between different types of authority, the effort to maintain the primacy of technical expertise in a research and development center such as Nampa may require continued use of structural changes. The Nampa plan may represent, therefore, not only the efforts of a new Director to assert his leadership, but also his efforts to prevent erosion of technical knowledge as a basis of power in the organization.

The relationship between types of authority in the organization and the individual synthesis in establishing power introduces elements of competition which go beyond the immediate formal organization structure. There are broader issues of conflict of interest between the organization and the individual which affect responses to initiations from the top of the hierarchy. The conflict of interest centers on change in power in the face of justifications for organizational change and the interaction of differing criteria of rationality in behavior.

RATIONALITY IN BEHAVIOR

Changes undertaken to benefit an organization, as in the Nampa case, have differential effects on individuals: some gain and others lose in power. This fact sets the stage for individual response to change. The problem is complicated by the fact that changes are presented in rational terms, with the organization as the point of reference for judging the appropriate relationship between ends sought and means used. The organization, however, does not speak for itself, but only in the voice of its chief executive. The issue of response to change therefore involves a strong element of personal relationship and communication, particularly at the higher levels of management.

One of the controversial issues in organization theory centers on the question of whether it is possible to create changes where everyone gains power while the effectiveness of the organization also increases.[5] If this notion smacks of utopianism, it is nevertheless a strong influence on current experimentation in organizations.

Suppose we visualize an organization with an infinite amount of authority to distribute to members; assume further no particular difficulties in settling on a rational procedure for distributing authority. Under these two conditions, it would seem possible to devise plans for enhancing authority of all individuals.

This speculation comes under question on the ground that the crucial issue affecting power is the relative distribution of authority. There are no absolute measures of authority, and like other social assets used in human exchange the comparisons of authority are more central to determining individual response than measures on absolute scales.

If an individual's authority remains constant while an organizational change increases the amount attached to other offices, then the individual will in all probability experience the change as a deprivation. Authority, like any other valued social commodity, is subject to comparisons of gains or losses in the proportions allocated.[§]

Judging the rationality of response to changes in the organization structure requires an assessment of alterations in the proportional distributions of authority. If change decreases an individual's proportional amount of authority, then it is rational for him to experience the shift as a deprivation and to resist the change through individual and collective

---

[§] DALTON-BARNES COMMENT: As was pointed out earlier, the assumption of a fixed sum of power and authority is not shared by all authors. Dismissing the arguments and findings of those who question this assumption (Tannenbaum and others) as utopian runs the risk of obscuring the point which is most vital to the understanding of power and authority in organizational change. This is the distinction between the *absolute* and *relative* amounts of power and authority. Tannenbaum argues that the total quantity of power (he uses the term control) can vary in an organization. If that, in fact, is the case, and Tannenbaum's data support his argument, conceivably everyone in an organization could gain power in absolute terms. But if all parties do not gain at an equal rate, some will sustain a relative loss. The tendency of individuals to use their associates and former peers as referents and rivals will push them toward using relative standards in assessing what has happened to them. This points up the difficulty of introducing change which will not be experienced by some parties as a loss of power. But difficulty and impossibility are not synonymous, and one of the most important tasks for research in this area is the identification of those conditions under which individuals are most likely to stress either absolute or relative standards. A beginning in this direction will be found in Chapter VII.

action. Resistance in such a case is no less rational than the justification for the change as a means of improving the organization's effectiveness.

There is no basis for assigning a higher value to rationality at the level of the organization than at the level of the individual. The situation is more accurately defined as a conflict of interest among members of an organization.

When conflict of interest occurs among individuals who have power, certain predictable behavior will occur among a series of alternatives: (1) the individuals will seek to enhance their power in responding to change through formation of coalitions; (2) with or without coalitions, bargaining, negotiation, or overt conflict will develop; (3) individuals in a condition of deprivation will leave the organization if bargaining is ineffective; or (4) individuals will adjust to lessened authority and power if alternative positions outside the organization are too costly to secure or are unavailable.

These four alternative actions are rational responses to change on the part of individuals. An irrational response is to act in any of these ways when a real deprivation does not occur or to fail to act in the face of real losses in relative authority.

Rationality at the level of individual response has a quality of concreteness not present in assessing rationality at the level of the organization. When the Director of Nampa presented his plan for change, the arguments offered to justify the new organization structure were two: (1) the need for change which would better enable the Center to translate its technical competence into marketable products; (2) the importance of increased participation in decisions and problem solving. While these were *plausible* arguments to justify the change, they were not *rational* in the logic of formal analysis which seeks to optimize the relationship between inputs and outputs.

Rationality in decision making exists when a relationship

of ends sought and means applied is optimal, given constraints and limits in assessing value of ends and means.[6] In organizational changes of a nontechnical nature, where measures of variables are not available, the relationship between ends and means is often vague. Rationalizations may be presented to justify change, but the case cannot be made for rationality in a strict sense.[§]

The issue which emerges is then persuasion to gain acceptance of change in the face of gains and losses in authority and power for specific individuals. Here, the individual's immediate experience with the change and the relative ease in judging its personal effects is compared with often vague and long-range effects for the organization. It is this context of comparison which leads to individual responses. Above all, the judgment of rationality of behavior does not depend on an absence of conflict with the organizational change and the proponents of change. Rationality and conflict are often companions in the relationships between the individual and the organization.

The most significant conflict of interest in the organizational change at Nampa was in the relationship between the Director and the Senior Managers. The supervisors whose jobs disappeared in the new plan had few alternatives to accepting the change. The Senior Managers could and did resist the change as a rational response to the plan. Their major attempts at resistance consisted of counter arguments

---

§ DALTON-BARNES COMMENT: Who is to say what "rationality in a strict sense" is, or that Dr. West's arguments were plausible but not rational "in the logic of formal analysis." March and Simon (1958) consider this view of rationality as one of the difficulties with classical theory. Their own more tolerant view of rational choice involved: (1) an approximate model of the real situation which they called the chooser's "definition of the situation," and (2) the definition coming from "psychological and sociological processes" including the chooser's own activities and the activities of others in his environment. Using this concept of rationality rather than the one drawn from classical economics, Dr. West's behavior was as rational as anyone else's in the Nampa situation.

to show weaknesses of the plan. There was no evidence to suggest attempts on their part to build coalitions with their subordinates to counter the change, or to appeal to higher management to exert pressure on the Director to modify his plan. Instead, the Senior Managers following vigorous presentation of their views accepted the plan with reservations. In the final analysis, the Senior Managers had limited power to stop or modify the change.

The main support for the change, beyond the willingness of individuals to go along with a top executive's program, came from Junior Managers and Senior Scientists for whom gains in authority and power appeared imminent. They had as a result a concordance of interests with the Director and could easily support his plan.

The other subordinates at levels below Junior Manager faced an interesting problem in gauging their response to change. For them, the plan could only arouse expectations that, for example, technical expertise had higher value in the new organization and their opportunity to contribute more directly in planning projects would increase.

But the effects of the change were least tangible for Junior Scientists: beyond increased expectations there was no immediate shift in behavior. Much depended on what the Junior Manager brought to the group from the outside and on his behavior as group leader. The new plan contained a general objective to involve Junior Scientists in decision making but no specific means for implementing this objective existed in the plan itself.

This interpretation of the position of Junior Managers in the change raises for consideration the rationale for equalization of authority as a means of improving organizational effectiveness. The Nampa case is one instance of a more general trend in organizations to equalize authority as a means of increasing the motivation to work and the value of contributions members make to organizations.

EQUALIZATION OF AUTHORITY

Appendix B reviews the methods used to equalize authority and power in organizations and the rationale in back of these methods. Beyond the particular approaches for achieving equalization there are broader structural and ideological issues to be considered. Equalization consists of any attempt to alter the proportional distributions of authority so that a relative shift occurs in favor of low ranking members of the hierarchy. The means for achieving this objective may be structural or ideological.§

Structural shifts are intended to increase organizational effectiveness through greater participation and work involvement. The acquisition of authority is supposed to enhance the individual's motivation to work. In addition, the new distribution usually aims at enhancing authority at levels appropriate to the techniques and operations of the organization. The structural approaches to specialization are therefore limited: only selected positions in the hierarchy have increased authority. In the Nampa case, the selective approach initially enhanced authority of Junior Managers and decreased authority of Senior and Middle Managers.

Examples of structural approaches to equalization are decentralization, establishment of profit centers, and use of task forces and standing committees. These methods for achieving equalization in a hierarchy occur most frequently in science-based organizations with large numbers of professional employees and in large-scale organizations where the problem of size demands multiple decision centers throughout the hierarchy.

---

§ DALTON-BARNES COMMENT: The equalization of power (or authority as used here) again assumes a closed system of power. This amounts to a zero-sum type game where one party's power is gained or lost at the expense of the other party's. The concept of power equalization ignores, however, the possibility of (and research on) non-zero-sum or mixed motive games where total power change may occur.

Ideological movements toward equalization are best known in the political sphere, but they have counterparts in industry. The distinguishing features of ideological approaches are their comprehensiveness and rationale. Instead of selectivity in equalization, the aim is toward larger and broader shifts to transfer authority from the top to the bottom of the hierarchy. Examples of ideological approaches to equalization include programs such as the Scanlon Plan, workers' councils, and various other approaches including certain aspects of the human relations and group dynamics movements.

The Nampa plan was clearly a structural approach to equalization. Its aims were pragmatic and its means selective even to the extent of establishing "control" groups to permit comparisons of the effects of change. The Nampa plan contained specific techniques for altering decision making and motivating professionals: the new organization chart with its revised job descriptions; the budgetary and project review discussions; the composition of work groups to include Senior Scientists; the CAPS committees to connect into the working structure of the Center outside groups such as sales and the research departments. All these techniques gave substantive means for transferring authority, none of which required alterations in beliefs and values. The critical issue in this experiment in equalization became therefore the efficacy of the shifts in improving the output of the Center.

Increases in output in research and development work depend upon selection of projects and bringing to bear technical knowledge in solving the problems inherent in the projects undertaken. Organizational experiments do not alter these requirements for successful technical work. People have to develop ideas, to know how to select from many alternatives for allocation of resources, and to apply intuition, knowledge, and experimentation in solving problems.

Equalization of authority in the particular program

adapted at Nampa was an indirect approach to increasing output. The Director assumed that the existing people in the organization and the mix of resources available were adequate to the project work of the Center. The limitation he attempted to overcome was in the application of effort and the locus of decision making in the old authority structure. If the professional staff was not adequate in expertise and experience to the type of technical work demanded in the projects, then it is difficult to see how equalization by itself would affect results materially. Or to take the opposite position, the improvement in quality of staff, ranging from Junior Scientists to Senior Managers, could conceivably increase productivity without any shifts in the authority structure.

There are reality considerations in work organization, such as quality of competence and availability of resources, which stand independent of organizational structure. Structural approaches to equalization may be significant to improving the uses of competence and application of resources, but they cannot transcend basic limitations in talent and expertise.

The measurement of capability and formal evaluations of professional staff were not undertaken prior to the introduction of the change in formal organization. Nor were there significant additions to the professional and managerial staffs. The experiment in equalization as a structural approach to increasing the Center's effectiveness is therefore uncontaminated from a research standpoint. The evaluation of the results of change, to follow in Chapter IV, will provide indications of how far equalization by itself can improve performance as perceived by members of the organization. It is important to bear in mind in interpreting the research results the range of reality factors besides the organizational structure which determine effectiveness.

CHAPTER IV

Results

PROFESSIONAL employees and managers in the Nampa Center completed two sets of questionnaires: the first before the implementation of the new organization structure and the second after 15 months of experience with the plan. [See Appendix A] Responses to the questionnaires provided the largest block of data for purposes of analyzing the effects of the change. A second body of data developed from interviews and the study of records over a three-year period following the introduction of the plan.

The data, which will be presented in detail in this chapter, show these results:

(1) Men in the experimental departments were more likely to report increases in work involvement and personal productivity than were their counterparts in comparative departments.

(2) There was, however, no overall shift in the number of men in either the experimental or comparative departments who were satisfied with the effectiveness of the Center in performing its task.

(3) The technical changes in authority structure altered the interaction and influence patterns in the experimental departments, in turn producing further changes in authority.

(4) Within the experimental departments, respondents who experienced an increase in authority evaluated the effects of the program more positively than those who experienced a reduction or no change.

(5) Regardless of the degree to which individuals had gained or lost authority, Managers as a whole were in favor of a halt to the changes, or at least a reduced rate of change,

while Scientists favored an acceleration and an extension of the program.

(6) Heightened expectations, triggered by the actual changes, resulted in dissatisfaction with superiors and a greater tendency to consider leaving the Center among respondents whose authority and influence remained unchanged.

The reader will observe in the following presentation of detailed results a difference in the magnitude of effect depending upon the type of question used in the analysis. In some cases, the data compare responses to the same question before and after the change, and in others present retrospective responses indicating the individuals' own appraisal of the change 15 months after the plan had been put into effect. The comparative results consistently show a small shift in attitude while the retrospective data show strong and more positive evaluations of involvement, satisfaction, and productivity. This difference results from the nature of the measurement and means that the two types of data cannot be treated as equivalents.* The patterns within each type of data can be compared, however, particularly in evaluation of the responses according to occupational group. Viewed in this way, the data present a coherent picture of the effects of change.

OVERALL MEASURES

Organizational change generally creates expectations of overall beneficial effects for the organization. In fact, since

---

* A recent study by Hardin demonstrates that retrospective and comparative data correlate positively but are not equivalent. A change of three points on a nine-point scale in a retrospective question related to a change of only one point in a comparative question. Comparative measures, on the other hand, have been repeatedly shown to be subject to a "regression effect." Items or responses which deviate sharply from the norm tend to move toward the mean in subsequent measures. See Hardin, "Perceived and Actual Change in Job Satisfaction," pp. 363–367; Guilford, *Psychometric Methods*, pp. 323–327; Lord, "Elementary Models for Measuring Change," pp. 21–25.

the Western Electric studies,[1] the so-called Hawthorne effect
has been interpreted by many to suggest that almost any
change indicating top management concern for the organization and its members will produce favorable results in productivity and satisfaction. Examination of overall effects in
this study shows the change produced nothing like a Hawthorne effect, at least as reflected in the judgments of the
respondents.

Table 1 presents data on the men's evaluation of the Center
as a competitive organization based on responses to a question asked before and after the change.

TABLE 1

PERCEIVED ORGANIZATIONAL EFFECTIVENESS

(Percentages of respondents who indicated they were satisfied with the
Nampa Center as a hard-hitting organization capable of competing
successfully with similar organizations in industry)

	N[a]	Before change	After change
All Respondents	153	51%	54%
Experimental Departments (CAPS)	72	57%	61%
Comparative Departments (Non-CAPS)	81	47%	48%

[a] A total of 153 scientists and managers participated in the study both
before and after the change. Minor variations in the total N in subsequent
tables results from missing or ambiguous responses to particular questions.

There was little change in the number of men in either
the experimental or the control groups who were satisfied
with the Center's effectiveness. While answers to before-after
questions tend toward conservative results, the data indicate clearly the absence of a halo effect in judging the effectiveness of the Center. Table 1 does show a stronger positive
evaluation in the experimental groups as compared with the
comparative groups before as well as after the change (Before $X^2 = 1.55$, $p < .15$; After $X^2 = 1.20$, $p < .15$). This
result probably stems from the tendency to select for change

those groups most central to the future of the organization and whose members are most committed to the organization. But whatever prior commitments, the change itself did not lead to a generalized optimism in their evaluation of the Center.

Table 2 presents the retrospective reports of the overall effects on work involvement while Table 3 compares the men's reported attitudes toward leaving the Center. These two tables indicate that members of experimental groups generally experienced the change with heightened involvement but, as its corollary, a somewhat stronger willingness to consider leaving Nampa for similar positions elsewhere.

TABLE 2

WORK INVOLVEMENT

Percentage reporting:

	N	Increased work involvement	Decreased work involvement	No change
All Respondents	136	40%	7%	53%
Experimental Departments	68	54%	9%	37%
Comparative Departments	68	26%	6%	68%

TABLE 3

ORGANIZATIONAL ATTRACTIVENESS

(Percentage reporting they would ignore job offers for similar position in other organizations)

	N	Before change	After change
All Respondents	152	86%	71%
Experimental Departments	72	90%	71%
Comparative Departments	80	81%	71%

The decrease in percentages of respondents willing to ignore job offers reflects a heightened restlessness and willingness to evaluate their continued participation in the organization. Both the before and after questions showed a low total percentage of men who would consider other offers. This is partly a result of the wording of the question, which was designed to test general restlessness and satisfaction apart from the prospect of increased rewards in a new organization. The shift in percentages between the before and after responses, however, with the men in the experimental departments more willing to test their continued participation in Nampa, indicates a heightened emotional engagement on the part of members closely involved in the change. This interpretation gains support from the results in Table 2. The retrospective report in Table 2 indicates a general increase in work involvement with a stronger trend in the case of the experimental groups ($X^2 = 9.18$, $p < .005$).

The fact that the change itself produced no overall halo effect in the experimental departments but instead a heightened involvement and a stronger willingness to look elsewhere suggests a relatively independent appraisal on the part of respondents. Changes set in motion heightened awareness along with fresh appraisals of work life. But changes do not always, or even usually, produce uniformly favorable effects. When a veteran of organization change reads of changes with uniformly positive results, he either marvels at their utopian success or regards the measures with silent skepticism. The absence of global optimism on the part of respondents at the Nampa Center seems not unrealistic on the whole, particularly in view of the fact that the changes in authority instituted at Nampa were technical and selective. The analysis of results by status level and occupational group will indicate the main points at which the change had its impact and with what types of effects.

DIFFERENTIATION BY ORGANIZATIONAL POSITION AND LEVEL

The changes instituted had been designed to affect the lives of men within the experimental departments in quite different ways. If authority was to be moved downward, senior men would be affected in a different way from junior men. If professional authority was to be enhanced, scientists might be expected to respond in a different way from managers. For purposes of analysis, therefore, the men at the Center were divided along three dimensions:

(a) by their membership in either an experimental or a comparative department, i.e.,
   (1) CAPS
   (2) Non-CAPS

(b) by the type of position held, i.e.,
   (1) Scientists
   (2) Managers

(c) by the level of their position, whether they had yet achieved senior management level or been promoted to Senior Scientist positions (this dimension did not reflect age but only position level), i.e.,
   (1) Junior
   (2) Senior

Eight categories resulted:

CAPS Junior Scientists	CAPS Senior Scientists
Non-CAPS Junior Scientists	Non-CAPS Senior Scientists
CAPS Junior Managers	CAPS Senior Managers
Non-CAPS Junior Managers	Non-CAPS Senior Managers

To look at specific rather than global outcomes for the men in each of these categories, the several types of outcomes sought by the Director will be examined separately. The first of these were specific changes in time allocation and interaction patterns. Second, these changes in behavior were to result in an alteration of authority relationships. Finally, shifts in authority relationships were intended to bring improvements in productivity and satisfaction.

Time Allocations and Interaction Patterns

One of the Director's explicit goals in the experimental groups was to reduce the amount of contact between the Senior Managers and those who reported to them (the Junior Managers and the Senior Scientists). He attempted to accomplish this largely by putting increased demands on the superior, leaving him little time to provide close and detailed supervision over his men. The CAPS Senior Managers were instructed to devote half their time to long-range technical planning for the Center and the Division, and only the remaining hours working with the men under them (the CAPS Junior Managers and Senior Scientists). Therefore, if the changes were to have their desired effect in this respect, Senior Managers in the experimental departments would spend less time with subordinates than before and more time in planning activities. Junior Managers would increase their contacts with outsiders. Senior Scientists would spend more time working directly with groups in the experimental departments. To what extent were these aims achieved?

Senior Managers and Long-Range Technical Planning

At the end of the 15-month period, there was unanimous agreement among all the men interviewed at the Center that the Senior Managers had devoted almost no time to long-range planning. Even the Director listed this as one of the things which had not yet been accomplished. He reported that he had had some limited success in "shaking the managers loose" but that the long-range planning had not begun.

One of the Junior Managers reported on the activities of the Senior Manager over him as follows:

> My boss, Orville, has three project groups under him and he still keeps abreast of all three. He doesn't sit in on the CAPS committee meetings, of course, but he hears about what happens in them afterward. The other Junior Man-

agers and I are somewhat on our own: we work out our own budgets, but we still work very closely with him on them, and he coordinates our activities with the overall plant budget. All our contact with Dr. West is still through Orville except for the CAPS reporting meetings. Orville spends more of his time away from the plant now than he did previously, but he still stays fairly close to our activities.

The Manager of Administrative Services similarly reported that the CAPS Senior Managers were not spending any time doing long-range planning:

In my opinion, there has been no more long-range planning done this year than in any previous year. From what I've seen of the Senior Managers this year, I would say that they haven't really changed their day-to-day way of doing business. If you had been sitting in my office and had looked through the glass window here into Dick West's office, watching those CAPS committee chairmen reporting to the Vice President every three weeks, you'd notice that every time a CAPS Junior Manager comes in, you can be damn sure his Manager is also present. You can't get long-range planning from a man if he stays that closely tied to day-to-day activities.

At times the Director himself questioned how realistic his own expectations had been, though he still felt that the plan could be made to work:

I am not sure that my plan to have the Senior Managers do long-range planning wasn't a dream. They didn't want that at all. It is difficult to be placed in an amorphous position with no direct responsibility. I have to admit that. Yet, I still think this planning has to be done.

The CAPS Senior Managers themselves reported that, with a new and demanding set of technical objectives being embarked upon in their departments, they had just not found the time to give to planning. Crises, missed deadlines, and interpersonal misunderstandings within their departments demanded their attention. The difficulties and uncertainties of establishing new, and as yet ambiguous, roles were unmentioned. But for whatever reason, they did not transfer their time to planning and therefore established no new contacts around planning activities. Consequently, any plans for them to exert influence in the planning sphere were, of necessity, unfulfilled. Whatever losses in contact or influence they might have absorbed had not been compensated for through planning.

Contact with Outsiders

A second intended change was to make the Junior Managers the major point of contact with outsiders concerned with work being done at the Center. This attempt was not new with the advent of the CAPS committees but had been tried before in various ways. However, previous to the introduction of the CAPS program, all such attempts had failed. Outsiders had continually shown a preference for working with Senior Managers. Junior Managers, knowing this, had been reluctant to push themselves into this role even when urged to do so. One of the Senior Managers commented on this reluctance:

> For at least three years management has been hounding the Junior Managers to go over to Research and Sales and communicate with the people over there. This was never very successful. It was very painful to hear management cry every three months that our Junior Managers never communicate with Research.

The pattern changed, however, when the Junior Managers' contacts with the outsiders were formalized through the regular CAPS committee meetings. These meetings effectively made the Junior Managers the outside contact men for the Center. Not only did the meetings establish contact between the Junior Managers and the outsiders, but the fact that the

Senior Managers were excluded from the meetings limited their knowledge about the project. All the men interviewed agreed that this objective had been successfully achieved. According to one of the Senior Managers:

> The Junior Managers have become the focal point for all outside contact. It used to be that people would always come to me if they had a problem concerning our department. Now they go to the Junior Manager. This is partly because of the fact that he is on the CAPS committee. But it also reflects the fact that I'm not as close to the work as I used to be. After someone came to me two or three times and I couldn't answer his questions, but had to refer him to the Junior Manager instead, it wasn't long until he started going to him directly.

Increased Utilization of Senior Scientists

A third objective of the program was an increase in the utilization of Senior Scientists. This included the few Senior Scientists who were assigned as regular members of the Project Groups in the experimental departments, but the primary objective was the better use of the Senior Scientists working in the staff specialist group. The many previous attempts to get the line groups to make effective use of these Senior Scientists had not been considered successful since the staff specialist group had been established.

This time, however, things were different. All the men interviewed at the end of the 15-month period agreed that there had been a significant increase in the use of the Senior Scientists. Under the new program, the utilization of these men had become almost exclusively an assignment of the Junior Managers. Nearly all the men interviewed reported that the Junior Managers had increased their contact with Senior Scientists and that they were leaning more heavily on their advice than had ever been the case when the Junior Managers were working closely under the Senior Managers. Conversely, the Senior Scientists in the staff specialist group generally agreed that it was a distinct advantage to them to be able to deal directly with the Junior Managers. Following are some of their comments:

> One of the changes that has taken place in our work is that instead of dealing with the Senior Managers, we have begun dealing directly with the Junior Managers. This has been a big help. It is amazing how much more detail you can get when you are dealing with the person who is doing the work.

*   *   *   *   *

> My supervisor has assigned several people to work closely with certain CAPS projects. I, myself, am working with three of them. If the Project Leader has an analytical problem, I am the liaison man with the staff analytical group. Even though I am not an expert in each of these areas, I am more of an expert than the Project Leader. After I become acquainted with his problem, I can direct him to the person who can do the best work for him.

Contact with Superiors

The above data, however, describe only contact with outsiders or with persons who were not in a hierarchical relationship to the men discussed. To see what changes, if any, had occurred in the amount of contact in the superior-subordinate relationships throughout the Center it is necessary to turn to the questionnaire data. Figure 6 indicates the changes in the number of men who reported daily contact with their immediate superior.

A simple bar chart has been used to indicate visually the proportionate change in each of the categories. It is necessary to keep in mind that the numbers are very different in these categories. The number of Senior Managers is small, and a change in the responses of one or two makes a much larger change in the bar chart for them than it does for Junior Scientists. But it is in the nature of organizations that there are fewer men at the top of the hierarchy than at the bottom. Therefore, if organizational position is used as an analytical category, we have to accept the fact of unequal numbers and take these into account in interpreting the data.

The data in Figure 6 do, in fact, indicate a greater reduction in superior-subordinate contact in the CAPS departments than in the Non-CAPS departments ($X^2 = 9.94$, p $< .005$). The intended reduction in the amount of contact between the CAPS Senior Managers and their subordinates (the CAPS Junior Managers and CAPS Senior Scientists) ap-

FIGURE 6

CHANGES IN THE FREQUENCY OF CONTACT WITH IMMEDIATE CHIEF

(Changes in the number of men who reported daily
contact with immediate chief)

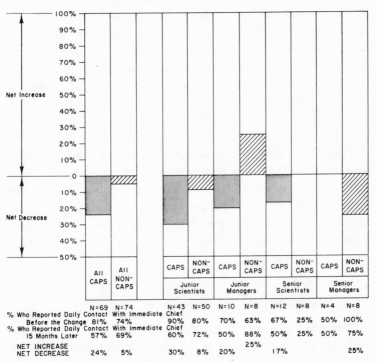

	All CAPS	All NON-CAPS	CAPS Junior Scientists	NON-CAPS Junior Scientists	CAPS Junior Managers	NON-CAPS Junior Managers	CAPS Senior Scientists	NON-CAPS Senior Scientists	CAPS Senior Managers	NON-CAPS Senior Managers
	N=69	N=74	N=43	N=50	N=10	N=8	N=12	N=8	N=4	N=8
% Who Reported Daily Contact With Immediate Chief Before the Change	81%	74%	90%	80%	70%	63%	67%	25%	50%	100%
% Who Reported Daily Contact With Immediate Chief 15 Months Later	57%	69%	60%	72%	50%	88%	50%	25%	50%	75%
NET INCREASE						25%				
NET DECREASE	24%	5%	30%	8%	20%		17%			25%

pears. (It does not appear in the reports of their counter-parts in the Non-CAPS departments.) But of all the groups, it was the CAPS Junior Scientists who were most likely to report a dwindling of contact between themselves and their chiefs, the CAPS Junior Managers ($X^2 = 7.82$, $p < .005$).

All four CAPS groups had experienced a diminution of contact in what had previously been significant superior-subordinate relationships. The Senior Managers did not report a reduction in contact with their superior, but their subordinates (the Junior Managers and Senior Scientists) reported a reduction in contact with them. The superior-subordinate contacts for all four groups had previously pro-vided settings where each superior and subordinate exerted influence, bringing to bear whatever authority and power he possessed. For members of two of these groups, the Junior Managers and the Senior Scientists, the new structure pro-vided them with the new contacts and new opportunities to influence others. Provisions had been made for them to work more closely with peers in the organization (the Senior Sci-entist with the Junior Managers and the Junior Managers with other members of the CAPS committees), and also with other supervisors in the organization (the Director and the Vice President).

The other two CAPS groups experienced the reduction in contacts with superiors and subordinates but were provided with no new contacts or settings in which these losses could be offset. New contacts connected with planning activities never materialized for the Senior Managers. The Junior Scientists were given nothing to replace their loss of contact with Junior Managers.

AUTONOMY AND POSITIONAL AUTHORITY

Frequency of contact and allocation of time, however, are only the quantitative part of the story. Even more important is what happened when supervisors and subordinates did come together. One of the stated aims of the program was to increase the amount of personal autonomy for the men at the Center — to increase the extent to which each person felt that he could exercise control over the manner in which he carried out his work.

Figures 7 and 8 give more information on the changes in the authority relationships at the Center. At the end of the 15 months, the men were asked to contrast the amount of autonomy and freedom they had at that time with the situation as it had existed 15 months earlier, and to make a sim-

FIGURE 7

REPORTED CHANGES IN AUTONOMY

(Retrospective reports)

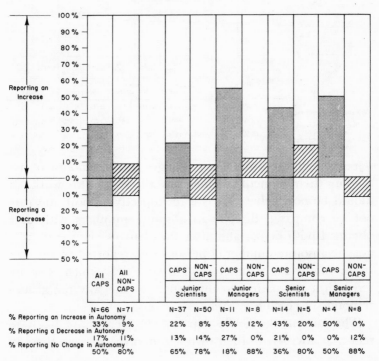

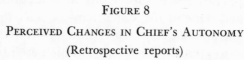

FIGURE 8

PERCEIVED CHANGES IN CHIEF'S AUTONOMY

(Retrospective reports)

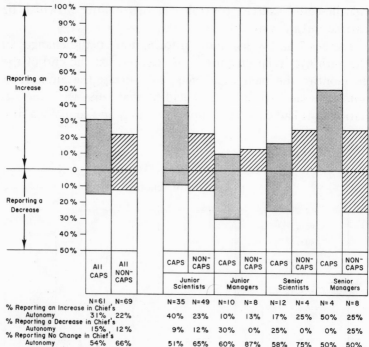

	All CAPS	All NON-CAPS		Junior Scientists		Junior Managers		Senior Scientists		Senior Managers	
				CAPS	NON-CAPS	CAPS	NON-CAPS	CAPS	NON-CAPS	CAPS	NON-CAPS
	N=61	N=69		N=35	N=49	N=10	N=8	N=12	N=4	N=4	N=8
% Reporting an Increase in Chief's Autonomy	31%	22%		40%	23%	10%	13%	17%	25%	50%	25%
% Reporting a Decrease in Chief's Autonomy	15%	12%		9%	12%	30%	0%	25%	0%	0%	25%
% Reporting No Change in Chief's Autonomy	54%	66%		51%	65%	60%	87%	58%	75%	50%	50%

ilar judgment regarding any changes in the amount of autonomy their immediate chief was allowed in his work. It should be noted that this is a retrospective report and cannot be compared directly in absolute numbers with data obtained both before and after the changes. However, it is not the absolute number of persons who reported an increase in autonomy for themselves or their chiefs which is of interest, but the patterned differences in the way the groups responded to each question.

The men in the CAPS departments were more likely to report an increase in their own autonomy than were those in

Non-CAPS departments ($X^2 = 11.78$, $p < .001$). However, this perceived increase in autonomy was not uniformly spread throughout the CAPS departments. The increased freedom reported by others in CAPS had not reached down to the same extent to the Junior Scientists. The CAPS Junior Scientists were less than half as likely as others in CAPS to report that their freedom to act had been increased ($X^2 = 4.69$, $p < .025$). Even though the CAPS Junior Scientists were the most likely to have lost contact with their superiors, they were the least likely to report an equivalent increase in freedom and autonomy. They reported increased autonomy for their immediate superiors, the CAPS Junior Managers, but not for themselves.

The CAPS Senior Managers at first present an enigma. Where previous data had suggested that their freedom to act was being restricted, two of the four reported increased autonomy. However, their self-reported increased autonomy was not corroborated by the reports of others. The men who reported to them, the CAPS Junior Managers and Senior Scientists, were less likely than others in CAPS to report an increase in their chief's autonomy ($X^2 = 3.50$, $p < .05$) and more likely to report that their chief had suffered a loss in autonomy ($X^2 = 2.35$, $p < .1$). Over a quarter of these men reported a decrease in the freedom allowed their chief, while this was true for less than 10% of the other respondents. Indeed, it is easy to imagine how being isolated from day-to-day demands might be described by a Senior Manager as bringing an increase in autonomy. But to others in the Center, this appeared to be not more autonomy, but less. To the men reporting to them, the changes had bound and restricted the Senior Managers' freedom to take action and use their capacities.

On the other hand, the other two CAPS groups, the CAPS Junior Scientists and the CAPS Senior Managers, were more likely than any others to report that their immediate supervisors had gained autonomy in the changes which had been made. In Chapter III hierarchical authority was pictured as moving both downward away from the Senior Managers to the Junior Managers and upward to the Director. The evidence here is that this shift was also observed by the men.

Interviews held with the men in the CAPS departments reveal a pattern very similar to that suggested by analysis of the questionnaire data. The CAPS Senior Managers, when asked about the effects of Dr. West's changes in organizational structure, talked primarily about the impact they saw on their subordinates rather than on themselves. On this topic they waxed enthusiastic:

> I believe that the biggest difference that has come about in day-to-day operations has been that greater responsibility has been pushed down to the Project Leaders. I have noticed in them more of a sense of urgency and a greater importance attached to their work than I ever did before.

*   *   *   *   *

> My impression is that the Project Leaders are taking a much more active part in what they now see as their own little business.

When asked about the effects on their own work at the Center, however, the CAPS Senior Managers had much less to say. One said he was pleased to be freed from some of the interruptions of outside contact and the detailed supervision of projects. He said he looked forward to getting into long-range planning, but had not been able to do so thus far. Another Senior Manager expressed his ambivalence:

SENIOR MANAGER:
> People in the CAPS program are better trained, I think. It has been very valuable to drop down the interface level of contact. It's developing group leaders who are more self-sustaining, more self-proficient. But the other side of the coin is that where I used to be a manager with three pro-

grams, now I have three guys with projects of their own. If I need to get a man away from one of these projects to help out with another, the head of the first project feels like I'm fouling *his* work.

INTERVIEWER:

It sounds like it's a little more uncomfortable to be a manager under this system.

SENIOR MANAGER:

You bet it is. There are a lot of meetings I can't go to. At these meetings there are decisions made that the manager isn't in on. So the responsibility for any failure must be diffused. Of course, I know I can still reverse some decisions, but if I do, I can kill the whole thing. You have to be subtle or you lose the whole show.

Still another Senior Manager denied that things had changed much at all:

When we talk about our "change in organization," I sort of rebel inside. I feel it denotes bigger differences than have actually taken place. We don't do things much differently in principle now than before. Responsibility and authority pass up the line as usual. I think it is more a difference in degree than in kind.

The Junior Managers described their increased autonomy as follows:

As far as I am concerned, I have more freedom and more decision-making responsibility than I ever had before.

* * * * *

Under this new setup, I have more to say about the direction of my people and about which particular project I want to emphasize on a certain day. I have certain goals which I have to meet, but there is no one breathing down my neck to tell me what to do each day. I am accountable for the overall group, but I have the discretion to concentrate on one aspect of our task and hold back on others.

This quotation is representative of a number of the comments made by Junior Managers during the last series of interviews: he talked about greater latitude for himself, but there is no mention of any change for the Junior Scientists who worked under him. He talked about having more freedom to direct the activities of the men in his group and more latitude to shift the efforts of his men from one activity to another, but there was little mention of the men under him sharing in these decisions.

All the CAPS Junior Managers did not share this attitude, however. One of them spoke at length about the opportunities and challenges he had tried to create for his subordinates:

> The CAPS program has been a big help to the young men in my group. It gives them more responsibility, and they have accepted it quite well. They go to some of the CAPS meetings and it gives them a good review of what is going on. I turned a part of the CAPS project over to one of the young men. I dropped it in his lap, and he has to sink or swim. I only act in an advisory capacity. He keeps me informed, and I can veto or suggest, but he has the complete responsibility. He works with the CAPS committee directly. He does things more by himself now. It used to be that I would be telling him what to do.

Not surprisingly, the Junior Scientist described in this quote reported having greater personal autonomy than he had had before the changes.

The experience of this one Junior Scientist, however, was not shared by most of the Junior Scientists. Several reported that they had not known initially that CAPS groups even existed. The first they knew about an actual change was when their group leader left to attend his first CAPS meeting. They reported that while their superior seemed to have more freedom to make decisions than before, things had changed very little for themselves. As one Junior Scientist put it:

> There really hasn't been much effect at all. I would say there has been no change, not only for my own group, but for other groups as well. . . . The changes don't seem to have penetrated as deeply as Dr. West hoped they would.

A little further information about the effect of the program on the Junior Scientists is given in Table 4, which re-examines some of the data already presented in Figure 7. Table 4, however, presents only the responses of the Junior Scientists to the question about changes in personal autonomy. The Junior Scientists are divided according to whether they had been assigned to a CAPS group, as well as whether, by their own report, their jobs had actually been affected by the CAPS program. Of the 37 Junior Scientists assigned to CAPS groups, close to half of them (16) reported that their jobs were not affected by the new program. Most of these 16 men were concentrated in groups working under Junior Managers who had apparently made little change in their relationships with subordinates. Only one of these 16 men reported any increase in his freedom to act. In most respects, the reports of these men were little different from

TABLE 4

CHANGES IN AUTONOMY REPORTED BY JUNIOR SCIENTISTS

	N	Percentage reporting an increase in personal autonomy
CAPS Junior Scientists reporting their jobs actually affected by CAPS	21	33%
CAPS Junior Scientists reporting their jobs not affected by CAPS	16	6%
All Non-CAPS Junior Scientists (those not assigned to CAPS groups)	50	8%

the Junior Scientists who had never been assigned to CAPS groups.

The structural changes introduced by the Director had had a strong impact on the authority relationships down through the Junior Managers, but had not assured any change below them. Implementing change in the Junior Manager's relationships with the Junior Scientists had been left largely up to the Junior Manager.

PROFESSIONAL AUTHORITY

We have seen evidence that positional authority had moved upward to the Director and down to the Junior Managers, but what of the intended increase in the use of professional authority? Had there been any change in the use of professional expertise as a basis for authority at the Center? For the CAPS Senior Scientists, at least, there does seem to have been a change. In the questionnaires, they reported greater autonomy than before in carrying out their work (Figure 7). In the interviews, the CAPS Senior Scientists and those who worked with them agreed that the Senior Scientists in the experimental departments were being more fully utilized and had more influence on the decisions being made at the Center. Interviews with the CAPS Senior Scientists were characterized primarily by the emphasis they placed on the increased opportunity they had to participate in problem solving.

> The sense of urgency that the CAPS program has given to the Junior Managers has helped us to get in on the project earlier than we had been able to before. It has given us a chance to show people that we can help them. Now, instead of getting requests to do small isolated parts of a problem, we have them coming to us and explaining their overall problem. We are getting more personally involved and becoming more of the problem-solving group.

*   *   *   *   *

Instead of the project leader coming to me and saying,

"Will you run this test and then give me the results?", I now become familiar with his problem and help him plan the kind of analytical work that needs to be done. The end result is that we do more problem solving. Another result is that staff people like myself are more aware of the results and of our effects on those results. Perhaps our efforts had helped solve the problem before, but we weren't aware of it. This is much more satisfying.

The CAPS Senior Scientists, according to their own reports and the reports of those around them, were clearly more influential, and whatever increased influence they had was, of necessity, based primarily on professional authority.

The Junior Scientists were a different matter, however. There was a fundamental difference in the situations under which the CAPS Senior Scientists and the CAPS Junior Scientists were operating. The Senior Scientists were primarily operating in a situation where there were no established superior-subordinate relationships. They were working largely with Junior Managers to whom they did not report. Moreover, these Senior Scientists were more specialized and could more nearly qualify as "professional experts." The Junior Scientists were still working directly under the Junior Managers, as they had previously. Almost half of them, as we saw, reported that their work had been unaffected by the program.

There was one interesting, if subtle, indication that professional authority had begun to make inroads on positional authority at the Center. The indicator derives more from the reports of the Managers than from the Scientists. Each of the respondents had been asked to make three judgments about the changes which had been instituted: (1) whether they felt the changes already made had had a beneficial effect on the Center; (2) whether there had been enough change thus far; and (3) whether they thought further changes were needed in the future. The distribution of the responses is shown in Table 5.

Table 5
Reactions to Past and Future Changes

		5A Those who felt that the changes had had a beneficial effect on the center		5B Those who felt there had been too little change thus far		5C Those who wanted further changes in the future	
		N	%	N	%	N	%
All Respondents	CAPS	66	65%	71	67%	67	58%
	Non-CAPS	67	62%	74	59%	73	55%
Junior Scientists	CAPS	39	54%	42	71%	38	66%
	Non-CAPS	43	63%	50	64%	48	64%
Junior Managers	CAPS	10	70%	11	63%	11	45%
	Non-CAPS	7	43%	6	33%	8	25%
Senior Scientists	CAPS	13	92%	14	64%	14	57%
	Non-CAPS	4	75%	6	83%	6	50%
Senior Managers	CAPS	4	75%	4	25%	4	25%
	Non-CAPS	13	54%	12	42%	11	36%
All Scientists		99	64%	112	68%	106	62%
All Managers		34	54%	33	47%	34	35%

Table 5 indicates that the CAPS Senior Scientists and the CAPS Junior Scientists were at opposite ends in their evaluation of the effects of the changes made thus far. Twelve of the 13 (92%) of the CAPS Senior Scientists felt that the changes already instituted were sufficient to have had a beneficial effect on the Center. Of the CAPS Junior Scientists, however, only about half (54%) felt that there had been enough change to have a positive effect.

Even though the CAPS Junior and Senior Scientists were the two groups farthest apart in their evaluation of the effects of the changes made (5A), their disagreement appears to stem primarily from the extent, rather than the kind, of the changes made. Scientists as a group were more likely than Managers to say the changes should be extended ($X^2 = 4.10$, $p < .025$). Among the CAPS groups, it was the Junior Scientists who were most likely to think that the changes had not gone far enough (5B). When we look at the question of further change in the future (5C), we find that both Junior and Senior Scientists wanted to extend what had been done more than did Managers ($X^2 = 7.10$, $p < .005$). This was true not only for those in CAPS but for the Non-CAPS Scientists as well. The one group which was most likely to criticize the changes for not having gone far enough was the Non-CAPS Senior Scientists (5B). They, like the CAPS Junior Scientists, had found themselves brushed by the changes which had restricted the exercise of positional authority and made possible the greater exercise of professional authority, but had not seen these changes affect their work. They had seen the CAPS Senior Scientists placed in a position where they could use their technical knowledge and expertise as a basis for exerting strong influence, but had not experienced it themselves. CAPS membership, in the responses to these questions, was not the differentiating factor that it was on questions about what had already happened at the Center.

Where the question concerned how the changes had affected the individual or his work, differences in response were, in large part, a function of whether or not the respondent was a member of CAPS and occupied a particular role therein. CAPS Junior Managers and CAPS Senior Scientists were most likely to respond in a similar manner. Managers as a group were not alike in their responses, nor were Scientists. Senior Managers did not respond the way Junior Managers did, nor did Junior Scientists follow the same pattern as the Senior Scientists. In the last two questions (5B and 5C) reported in Table 5, however, the Non-CAPS people were talking, not about their own jobs, but about what they had seen taking place in the experimental departments and were indicating whether they would like to see similar changes instituted in their own departments.

In their reactions to an extension of the changes, all the Managers tended to respond alike. CAPS Managers, both Junior and Senior, were likely to judge the changes thus far as beneficial to the Center, even though the Non-CAPS Managers were not so willing to concede this. But when it came to the question of carrying things even further in the direction already begun, the CAPS Junior Managers began to lose some of the enthusiasm, and the difference between Managers and Scientists becomes very apparent. They had seen what had happened to the authority of the CAPS Senior Managers, and they were apprehensive about the ultimate effect on positional authority in general. If enhancing the exercise of professional authority at the expense of positional authority had been insufficient to satisfy the Junior Scientists, it had at least been sufficient to cause concern and apprehension among the Managers about further change.

PERFORMANCE

The next question concerns performance, both organiza-

tional and individual. The changes in organizational structure had clearly altered time allocation and interaction
patterns and had effected a redistribution of authority and influence at the Center. But what effect had these, in turn,
on work performance? Central to the Director's objective was
an increase in organizational and individual effectiveness.

The data presented are the judgments of the men at the
Center concerning their own and each others' changes in
performance, and are not intended as an answer to the
question, "What changes in actual performance effectiveness had occurred?" Unfortunately, the nature of research
and development work does not lend itself to satisfactory
measures which could compare objectively levels of performance. [See note at end of chapter] The available data
do address a more modest but more answerable question
than the one above, i.e., "Was there a change in the men's
judgments of their own performance and in that of the
men around them?" Again, the significance of the reports
does not lie in the overall average of the self-reports, but
rather in the patterning of the changes evidenced in the eight
groups.

Personal Productivity Gains

Consider first what the men had to say about their own
personal productivity and that of their work group. Figure
9 summarizes the men's retrospective statements in response
to questions asking them to compare their current productivity with their output during a period prior to CAPS.
Figure 10 summarizes the responses to a similar question
concerning their group's productivity.

The men in CAPS departments were more likely to report
an increase in personal productivity than were the men in
comparative departments ($X^2 = 7.12$, $p < .005$). Within
CAPS the Junior Scientists indicated some increase, but it
was the Junior Managers and Senior Scientists within the

experimental departments who were most likely to report
an increase ($X^2 = 2.71$, p < .05). These were the same two
groups whose members had been most likely to report an
increase in autonomy.

When the patterns of responses to the two questions reported in Figures 9 and 10 are compared, one further finding
is revealed. The only men who were less likely to report
an increase in their group's productivity than in their own
personal ouptut were the CAPS Junior Managers and CAPS
Junior Scientists. The men in all the other categories were
as likely to report a gain in their group's output as in their

FIGURE 9

REPORTED CHANGES IN OWN PRODUCTIVITY

(Retrospective reports)

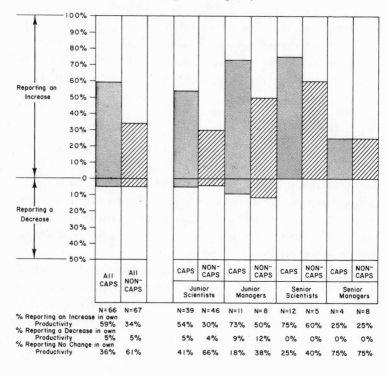

	All CAPS	All NON-CAPS	Junior Scientists		Junior Managers		Senior Scientists		Senior Managers	
			CAPS	NON-CAPS	CAPS	NON-CAPS	CAPS	NON-CAPS	CAPS	NON-CAPS
	N=66	N=67	N=39	N=46	N=11	N=8	N=12	N=5	N=4	N=8
% Reporting an Increase in own Productivity	59%	34%	54%	30%	73%	50%	75%	60%	25%	25%
% Reporting a Decrease in own Productivity	5%	5%	5%	4%	9%	12%	0%	0%	0%	0%
% Reporting No Change in own Productivity	36%	61%	41%	66%	18%	38%	25%	40%	75%	75%

Figure 10

Reported Changes in Group Productivity

(Retrospective reports)

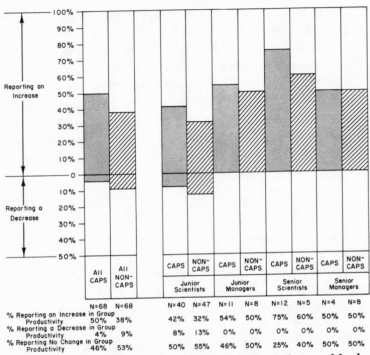

			CAPS	NON-CAPS	CAPS	NON-CAPS	CAPS	NON-CAPS	CAPS	NON-CAPS
	All CAPS	All NON-CAPS	Junior Scientists		Junior Managers		Senior Scientists		Senior Managers	
	N=68	N=68	N=40	N=47	N=11	N=8	N=12	N=5	N=4	N=8
% Reporting an Increase in Group Productivity	50%	38%	42%	32%	54%	50%	75%	60%	50%	50%
% Reporting a Decrease in Group Productivity	4%	9%	8%	13%	0%	0%	0%	0%	0%	0%
% Reporting No Change in Group Productivity	46%	53%	50%	55%	46%	50%	25%	40%	50%	50%

own. But the men in those two categories, who could observe firsthand what was happening in the Project Groups (made up largely of CAPS Junior Scientists), saw something in their groups which made them think the group had shown less improvement than they themselves had. It is not unlikely that this difference is a reflection of the fact that there were a number of Junior Scientists whose work had been untouched by the CAPS program. The data seen earlier indicated that the Junior Scientists were the members in the CAPS departments who had been least affected by the change in authority structure, and we see here a suggestion from their own reports and from those who observed them that their work output was also relatively unchanged.

The only CAPS group reporting less individual than group improvement was the CAPS Senior Managers. Two of the four concluded that their departments had increased productiveness, but only one of the four saw any gain in his own personal output. Thus, the comparison of the two tables demonstrates an internal consistency in the data on productivity. The two CAPS groups who were least likely to report personal productivity gains were the Senior Managers and Junior Scientists. The men who worked with the Junior Scientists saw the total group as less productive than themselves, and the Senior Managers saw their departments exceeding their own gains.

Organizational Effectiveness

The next question is, how did the men view what had happened to the Development Center as a whole? In Figure 1 it was found that when the reports of all the men were considered together, it appeared as if the men saw very little, if any, change in the organization's performance. Even when the men were divided into CAPS and Non-CAPS, no change in their view of the Center as a "capable, hard-hitting organization" was evident in either group. Our analysis of responses to other questions has established, however, that membership in CAPS versus Non-CAPS departments as a single variable was too gross a distinction and it masked an important pattern. Different groups in the CAPS departments were affected in quite different ways. Figure 11, therefore, reports the same information presented in Figure 1, but with the responses of Managers and Scientists (Junior and Senior) shown separately.

Note that Figure 11 reports comparative rather than retrospective data. The absolute amount of reported change,

FIGURE 11

PERCEIVED CHANGES IN ORGANIZATIONAL EFFECTIVENESS

(Changes in the percentage of men who said they were satisfied with the Nampa Development Center as a hard-hitting organization, capable of competing successfully with similar organizations in industry)

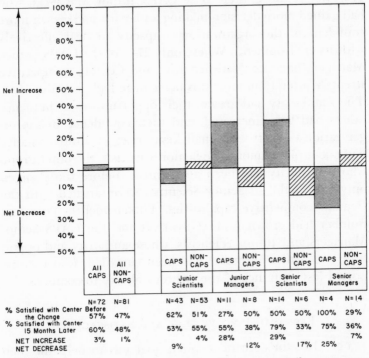

	All CAPS	All NON-CAPS	CAPS	NON-CAPS	CAPS	NON-CAPS	CAPS	NON-CAPS	CAPS	NON-CAPS
			Junior Scientists		Junior Managers		Senior Scientists		Senior Managers	
	N=72	N=81	N=43	N=53	N=11	N=8	N=14	N=6	N=4	N=14
% Satisfied with Center Before the Change	57%	47%	62%	51%	27%	50%	50%	50%	100%	29%
% Satisfied with Center 15 Months Later	60%	48%	53%	55%	55%	38%	79%	33%	75%	36%
NET INCREASE	3%	1%		4%	28%		29%			7%
NET DECREASE			9%			12%		17%	25%	

therefore, is much smaller than in the retrospective reports, though the pattern is similar.

The CAPS Junior Managers and Senior Scientists had developed a higher regard for the Center's capacity to produce and compete; CAPS Senior Managers and Junior Scientists were no longer so confident as they had been before. This pattern could be a resultant, at least in part, of the regression effect which is a characteristic of before-after questionnaire responses. The CAPS Junior Managers and Senior Scientists had been among the strongest critics of the Center in the first questionnaire. The CAPS Senior Managers and Junior Scientists had been among the most satisfied at that time, but the changes reflected in Figure 11 also parallel the redistribution of authority and the control of the decision-making processes at the Center. The CAPS Junior Managers, who had gained more decision-making authority, had grown more confident of the organization's capacity to deal effectively with its environment. Where only 27% of the CAPS Junior Managers had been satisfied with the Center's competitive strength, after 15 months this percentage had grown to 55%. Their authority had grown, their opportunities to influence others had been increased, and their confidence in the organization's effectiveness had kept pace. A similar change had taken place among the Senior Scientists, the other group whose authority had been augmented. Before the changes, only half of the 14 Senior Scientists were satisfied with the Center's competitive capabilities. Fifteen months later that number had grown to 11 (79%). It was the CAPS Senior Managers and Junior Scientists, whose authority and opportunity to utilize authority had been curtailed, who now reported less assurance of the Center's ability to compete.

Personal Involvement and Satisfaction

The Director's second explicit goal was to help the men find greater involvement and satisfaction in their work at the Center. He constantly pointed out to others that by satisfaction he did not mean complacency or acceptance of things as they were, but satisfaction with the Center as a place which offered challenging work, a promising future, and an opportunity to use their talents. He wanted to make the Center attractive enough to draw capable young men and hold the experienced men already there.

To examine changes in satisfaction, we will look at three

aspects of the men's experience at the Center: (1) satisfaction with the work, (2) satisfaction with the supervision, and (3) satisfaction with the Center as a place at which to pursue their careers. The data available on these aspects are of several kinds, posing again the problem and the opportunity of comparing data gathered in different ways. The retrospective reports of the men show a general increase in satisfaction and involvement in their work. The before-after data, which concern satisfaction with supervision and the Center as a place to work, show no such overall gain. Because of the differences in the way the data were elicited, comparisons of the absolute amounts of change are not valid. It is not possible, for example, to compare directly the changes in the men's satisfaction with their work with changes in their attitudes toward supervision. But internal comparisons of these data are possible and the comparison reveals the same pattern found earlier.

Satisfaction and Involvement in the Work

The men were asked, retrospectively, two questions about their work: (1) whether they found themselves more, or less, involved in their work than they had been before the CAPS program, and (2) whether they now found their work more, or less, satisfying. The responses are shown in Figures 12 and 13.

CAPS personnel were significantly more likely than Non-CAPS to report both increased involvement and satisfaction in their work (Involvement $X^2 = 9.18$, $p < .005$; Satisfaction $X^2 = 3.17$, $p < .05$). Among CAPS personnel, the Junior Managers and Senior Scientists were more likely to report increased involvement in their work than were Junior Scientists and Senior Managers ($X^2 = 3.08$, $p < .05$). A similar pattern is shown in the responses to the question about the satisfaction with their work, Figure 13, except for a somewhat different response from the CAPS Junior Managers.

FIGURE 12

REPORTED CHANGES IN WORK INVOLVEMENT

(Retrospective reports)

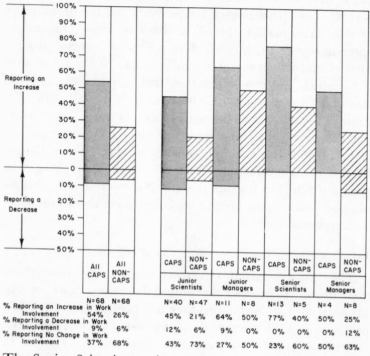

	All CAPS	All NON-CAPS		CAPS	NON-CAPS	CAPS	NON-CAPS	CAPS	NON-CAPS	CAPS	NON-CAPS
				Junior Scientists		Junior Managers		Senior Scientists		Senior Managers	
	N=68	N=68		N=40	N=47	N=11	N=8	N=13	N=5	N=4	N=8
% Reporting an Increase in Work Involvement	54%	26%		45%	21%	64%	50%	77%	40%	50%	25%
% Reporting a Decrease in Work Involvement	9%	6%		12%	6%	9%	0%	0%	0%	0%	12%
% Reporting No Change in Work Involvement	37%	68%		43%	73%	27%	50%	23%	60%	50%	63%

The Senior Scientists again stand out, but this time without the CAPS Junior Managers.

With all their other positive responses toward the change, it is somewhat surprising to find that the CAPS Junior Managers did not stand out in the amount of increased satisfaction they found in their work. The interviews with these men, however, suggest that this moderate rise in work satisfaction is consistent with their positive reports on other aspects of the changes (providing autonomy, involvement, etc.) and that the explanation lies in their experience in the CAPS committee meetings. The CAPS Junior Managers

FIGURE 13

REPORTED CHANGES IN WORK SATISFACTION

(Retrospective reports)

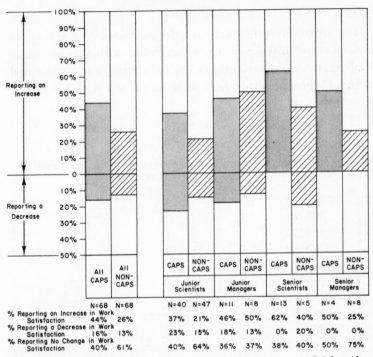

			CAPS	NON-CAPS	CAPS	NON-CAPS	CAPS	NON-CAPS	CAPS	NON-CAPS
	All CAPS	All NON-CAPS	Junior Scientists		Junior Managers		Senior Scientists		Senior Managers	
	N=68	N=68	N=40	N=47	N=11	N=8	N=13	N=5	N=4	N=8
% Reporting an Increase in Work Satisfaction	44%	26%	37%	21%	46%	50%	62%	40%	50%	25%
% Reporting a Decrease in Work Satisfaction	16%	13%	23%	15%	18%	13%	0%	20%	0%	0%
% Reporting No Change in Work Satisfaction	40%	61%	40%	64%	36%	37%	38%	40%	50%	75%

enjoyed their greater authority and influence within the Center. Many also found their new contacts with outsiders satisfying. A number, however, found it discomfiting to work within the CAPS committees where there was no hierarchical structure and where the use of positional authority was not legitimate. The same factor which was a source of satisfaction to the Junior Managers in one setting (i.e., their increased ability to influence others at the Center on the basis of positional authority) was also an offsetting source of dissatisfaction to some of them in the CAPS committee meetings (i.e., inability to influence on the basis of positional authority). For other Junior Managers who were comfortable with developing power derived from other sources, the CAPS committees were a satisfying experience.

Satisfaction with Immediate Chief

The next question examines the reactions of the men to the changes instituted in superior-subordinate relations. Each man was asked both at the beginning and at the end of the 15-month period how satisfied he was with his imme-

FIGURE 14

REPORTED CHANGES IN SATISFACTION WITH IMMEDIATE CHIEF

(Changes in the percentage of men who reported high satisfaction with their immediate supervisor)

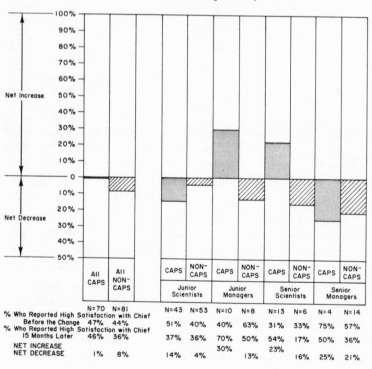

	All CAPS	All NON-CAPS	Junior Scientists		Junior Managers		Senior Scientists		Senior Managers	
			CAPS	NON-CAPS	CAPS	NON-CAPS	CAPS	NON-CAPS	CAPS	NON-CAPS
	N=70	N=81	N=43	N=53	N=10	N=8	N=13	N=6	N=4	N=14
% Who Reported High Satisfaction with Chief Before the Change	47%	44%	51%	40%	40%	63%	31%	33%	75%	57%
% Who Reported High Satisfaction with Chief 15 Months Later	46%	36%	37%	36%	70%	50%	54%	17%	50%	36%
NET INCREASE					30%		23%			
NET DECREASE	1%	8%	14%	4%		13%		16%	25%	21%

diate chief. Figure 14 presents the proportion of the men who indicated high satisfaction with their immediate chief both before and after the changes.

The total number registering high satisfaction with immediate chief was almost the same after the changes as before — even slightly lower. This was true not only for Non-CAPS, where there was no specific attempt to induce change, but for CAPS personnel as well. However, when the responses of the men in each category are separated, they follow a pattern similar to the retrospective reports on satisfaction. Among both the CAPS Junior Managers and Senior Scientists there was a net gain in the number reporting high satisfaction with their immediate superior. Among the other two CAPS groups, there was a net loss. The answers to this question have an interesting parallel in answers to the previous question about immediate chief, in which the men were asked whether their immediate superior had gained greater autonomy during the period of study. The subordinates of these men reported that the CAPS Junior Managers and the Director had gained autonomy but that the CAPS Senior Managers now had less freedom to act. Here, subordinates report greater satisfaction with the CAPS Senior Managers, whose autonomy and freedom to act, according to their report, had been restricted. Was this because they had gained what the Senior Managers had lost? What of the lowered satisfaction among the men who worked under the Junior Managers and the Director? What relationship does this have to the reports of these men that their bosses now enjoy greater autonomy? Did they feel that the gain had been at their expense? These data do suggest that some of these men, at least, were thinking in zero-sum terms: where one person gains, someone else loses. But such an explanation of their attitudes is too simple and leaves out the question of expectation. This issue will be reconsidered after an examination of the way in which expectations have affected the data in this study.

Satisfaction with the Center

One indication of satisfaction with the organization is the willingness of the members to leave. If a man is finding satisfaction in his work and sees an attractive future within the organization, the presumption could be made that he would be relatively unwilling to leave without strong inducement. On the other hand, if these things were not present, such strong inducements would be unnecessary to pull him away. On the basis of that presumption, each man was asked how seriously he would consider leaving if another organization were to offer him a position with about the same formal responsibilities and rewards he had at the Nampa Center. The overall response to this question was reported in Table 1, but Figure 15 records separately the percentage of men in each category who said they would ignore such an offer.

Managers in general were much less willing than Scientists to consider moving ($X^2 = 11.20$, $p < .001$). Thirty-five of the 37 Managers said they would not be interested in such an offer. But this had also been true before the changes. Most of the Managers felt sufficient attachment to the organization that they said they were willing to ignore outside job offers both before and after the changes, if it involved no advancement. The two who *were* looking around had been doing so before the study began. A different pattern appears among the Scientists, however. There were several who changed their reply to this question during the 15 months. The conditions under which they worked did appear to make a difference in the Scientists' willingness to stay with the organization. They were less willing than Managers to commit themselves to Nampa both before the changes, when 83% said they would ignore such an offer, and 15 months later when only 65% would. This drop occurred primarily among the CAPS Junior Scientists and the Non-CAPS Senior Scientists. These two groups had felt the peripheral

FIGURE 15

PERCEIVED CHANGES IN ORGANIZATIONAL ATTRACTIVENESS

(Changes in the percentages of respondents who said they would ignore job offer for similar positions in other organizations)

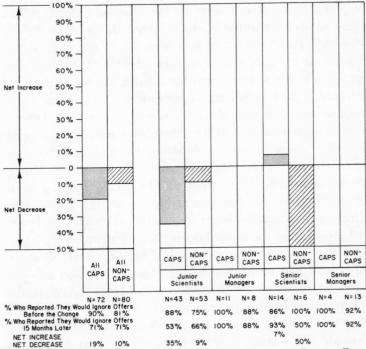

	All CAPS	All NON-CAPS		CAPS	NON-CAPS	CAPS	NON-CAPS	CAPS	NON-CAPS	CAPS	NON-CAPS
				Junior Scientists		Junior Managers		Senior Scientists		Senior Managers	
	N=72	N=80		N=43	N=53	N=11	N=8	N=14	N=6	N=4	N=13
% Who Reported They Would Ignore Offers Before the Change	90%	81%		88%	75%	100%	88%	86%	100%	100%	92%
% Who Reported They Would Ignore Offers 15 Months Later	71%	71%		53%	66%	100%	88%	93%	50%	100%	92%
NET INCREASE								7%			
NET DECREASE	19%	10%		35%	9%				50%		

effects of the change, but they had found no direct effect forthcoming in their own situation. Expectations had been raised but not fulfilled. The CAPS Senior Scientists had realized the gains in authority and influence the Director had promised, while in contrast the CAPS Junior Scientists had been promised, implicitly at least, similar gains, but had failed to realize them. The Non-CAPS Senior Scientists apparently compared themselves directly with the CAPS Senior Scientists and felt disadvantaged. An increased willingness to leave the Center seems to have been the consequence in both cases.

Expectation and Redefinition

This returns to the problem of raised expectations and their effect on all the data examined. The findings in this chapter thus far indicate that the Director had indeed reached a part of his goals at the Nampa Center. In the eyes of those who had gained what they had been led to expect from the changes in the authority structure (the CAPS Junior Managers and CAPS Senior Scientists) Nampa had become a more productive and satisfying organization. The outcomes of the changes were viewed with less enthusiasm by CAPS Senior Managers, who had had their own influence reduced. However, there is some indication that this had been expected by the Senior Managers from the time the changes were announced. The extent to which CAPS Senior Managers had believed that this reduction would be offset by other gains was difficult to determine. But the men who had grown most dissatisfied during the 15 months were those who had come to expect gains but had not realized them, those who had been close to the changes but had not participated in them. A significant number of CAPS Junior Scientists, in particular, indicated in a variety of ways that they were less satisfied with the Nampa Center after the changes than before they were instituted. Part of this disappointment seems due to their expectations that they too would now play an increased role in the decision-making connected with their work. Those expectations were realized in groups where the Junior Manager voluntarily adapted his working relationships to recognize professional authority more fully as a legitimate basis of influence. There had been no structural change which required him to do so, however, and most of the Junior Managers did not make such a change.

The differential outcomes for Junior Scientists in reported productivity, personal involvement, and satisfaction are shown in Table 6, which presents the responses of Junior

Scientists to four questions examined previously, but further divides them into three categories: (1) CAPS Junior Scientists who said their jobs had been affected by the CAPS program; (2) CAPS Junior Scientists who said their jobs *had not* been affected by the CAPS program; (3) Non-CAPS Junior Scientists. CAPS Junior Scientists who reported their

TABLE 6

INCREASES IN PRODUCTIVITY AND SATISFACTION REPORTED BY JUNIOR SCIENTISTS

Percentages of Junior Scientists
who reported an increase in:

	N	*Their own productivity*	*Their group's productivity*	*Their involvement in their work*	*Their satisfaction in their work*
CAPS Junior Scientists reporting their jobs actually affected by CAPS	23	65%	61%	56%	52%
CAPS Junior Scientists reporting their jobs not affected by CAPS	17	35%	18%	29%	18%
All Non-CAPS Junior Scientists (those not assigned to CAPS groups)	47	30%	32%	21%	21%

jobs had been affected in some way by CAPS were more likely than other Junior Scientists to report increases in personal productivity ($X^2 = 6.20$, $p < .01$), group's productivity ($X^2 = 6.44$, $p < .01$), involvement ($X^2 = 7.05$, $p < .005$), and work satisfaction ($X^2 = 6.91$, $p < .005$). Junior Scientists who were assigned to CAPS groups but who reported that their jobs were not affected by the program differed little from those in Non-CAPS departments.

The fact that over a third of the CAPS Junior Scientists reported that the program had not affected their jobs helps explain why they were less likely to report increases in productivity and satisfaction than were the CAPS Senior Scientists and CAPS Junior Managers. But what of the findings in Figures 14 and 15 that the CAPS Junior Scientists were even more likely than the Non-CAPS Junior Scientists to become dissatisfied with their chief and with the Center? Supposedly, none of the Non-CAPS people had their jobs affected by the CAPS program, while two-thirds of the CAPS Junior Scientists reported at least some change.

Table 7 provides a tabulation of the responses of Junior Scientists only to the questions concerning changes in satisfaction with immediate chief and willingness to consider offers from other firms. Thirty per cent of the non-affected CAPS Junior Scientists indicated a lowered satisfaction with their immediate supervisor. This one group of non-affected CAPS Junior Scientists accounted for nearly half the men in the Center whose statements indicated they had grown dissatisfied with their immediate chief. This group also included nearly half the men at the Center who had indicated an increased willingness to consider leaving the Center, though in this case it was not just the non-affected CAPS Junior Scientists, but some affected CAPS Junior Scientists who had begun to consider leaving.

Thus the instances of increased dissatisfaction were centered in the CAPS Junior Scientists group, primarily among those who said their work had not been affected, but also among the Junior Scientists who felt their work had been affected by the program, but not enough or not in the right way. Why was the dissatisfaction concentrated in this group?

The answer apparently lies in unfulfilled expectations. To illustrate, it will be necessary to examine the responses to one more set of questions. Table 8 compares the responses of CAPS and Non-CAPS Junior Scientists to questions about

TABLE 7

CHANGES IN SATISFACTION WITH IMMEDIATE
CHIEF AND WITH THE CENTER REPORTED BY
JUNIOR SCIENTISTS

	7A		7B	
	N	*Percentage decrease in number of Junior Scientists indicating high satisfaction with immediate chief*	N	*Percentage decrease in number of Junior Scientists indicating they would ignore job offers for similar positions in other firms*
CAPS Junior Scientists reporting their jobs actually affected by CAPS	23	0%	23	30%
CAPS Junior Scientists reporting their jobs not affected by CAPS	20	30%	20	40%
All Non-CAPS Junior Scientists (those not assigned to CAPS groups)	53	4%	53	9%

their preferred and actual relationship with their immediate supervisors when determining what concrete work problems or assignments or follow-up steps to work on next. Table 8 divides the responses of the men between those who reported that these decisions were usually made either by themselves or jointly with their chief, versus those who reported that the chief actually made these decisions. Before the changes, approximately the same percentage of CAPS (40%) and Non-CAPS (38%) Junior Scientists reported that

TABLE 8

JUNIOR SCIENTISTS' REPORTS OF ACTUAL AND PREFERRED RELATIONS
WITH CHIEF IN DAY-TO-DAY DECISIONS

(Percentage who indicated chief actually makes decisions)

	N	Before change	After change
CAPS Junior Scientists	40	40%	35%
Non-CAPS Junior Scientists	52	38%	61%

(Percentage who indicated they preferred to have chief make decisions)

	N	Before change	After change
CAPS Junior Scientists	43	14%	12%
Non-CAPS Junior Scientists	51	23%	43%

the chief made these decisions for them. Fifteen months later, the CAPS Junior Scientists tended to answer the question the same way, but this was not true for the Non-CAPS men. The percentage of Non-CAPS Junior Scientists who said that the chief was the one who, on a day-to-day basis, decided which problem and which follow-up steps to take jumped from 38% to 61% ($X^2 = 4.47$, $p < .025$).

Why, then, did not the Non-CAPS Junior Scientists change their attitude toward their immediate chief? Why did the CAPS rather than the Non-CAPS Junior Scientists become more dissatisfied? The answer is suggested in Table 8 concerning the kind of relationship the men preferred with their boss. Again, no change appears among the CAPS Junior Scientists, but 20% of the Non-CAPS Junior Scientists had shifted, stating that they now preferred to have their chief make the decisions ($X^2 = 3.51$, $p < .05$).

There are a number of possible explanations for these data, of course. Taking Table 8 alone, one might conclude that the Non-CAPS Junior Managers had shifted their style of leadership toward more centralized decision making and that their men had shifted their preferences to coincide with that shift. All our other data, however, suggest that the primary changes at the Center had not occurred in the relationship between the Non-CAPS Junior Scientists and their chiefs but between those in the CAPS departments.

A second possible explanation is that the differences in the responses reported in Table 8 could have been accounted for by differences in the individual predispositions of the two groups of Junior Scientists. Vroom, in a study of reactions to various supervisory styles, found that participation in decision making had positive effects on attitudes only among men with certain personality characteristics. Those people whom he defined as authoritarians or people without strong needs for independence were relatively unaffected by opportunity to participate.[2] If the Non-CAPS Junior Scientists were more "authoritarian" and began to see management allowing subordinates greater participation in decision making, they could naturally be expected to be less attracted to such a change than were others. This was tested by the use of the measure used by Vroom to determine authoritarianism — the California F-Scale. Table 9 divides the Junior Scientists according to their score on the F-Scale as well as on their responses to the questions on actual and preferred relations with chief in day-to-day decisions.

There was a very small tendency for the Non-CAPS Junior Scientists to be higher on the authoritarianism scale than were the CAPS Junior Scientists (58% of Non-CAPS were high scorers versus 47% CAPS) ($X^2 = .783$, $p < .25$). Furthermore, within the CAPS–Non-CAPS categories, the high scorers did show a greater preference for decisions to be made by the chief than did low scorers (Before $X^2 = 1.42$,

TABLE 9

JUNIOR SCIENTISTS' REPORTS OF ACTUAL AND PREFERRED RELATIONS
WITH CHIEF IN DAY-TO-DAY DECISIONS —
DIVIDED BY F-SCALE SCORE

(Percentage who indicated chief actually makes decision)

	N	*Score on F-Scale*	*Before* change	*After* change
CAPS Junior Scientists	20	High authoritarian	40%	45%
	23	Low authoritarian	35%	26%
Non-CAPS Junior Scientists	30	High authoritarian	43%	60%
	22	Low authoritarian	32%	64%

(Percentage who indicated they preferred chief to make decision)

	N	*Score on F-Scale*	*Before* change	*After* change
CAPS Junior Scientists	20	High authoritarian	20%	15%
	23	Low authoritarian	9%	9%
Non-CAPS Junior Scientists	30	High authoritarian	27%	52%
	22	Low authoritarian	18%	32%

$p < .15$; After $X^2 = 5.16$, $p < .025$). But these two tendencies
still do not help account for the fact that both high and low
scoring Non-CAPS Junior Scientists showed a greater preference for decisions by chief after the changes than before,
while this was not true for either high or low scoring CAPS
Junior Scientists.

The most economical explanation, in view of the other
data, is that the changes which had taken place in the CAPS
program, particularly among the Senior Scientists, had led
to a redefinition of influence. The criteria for determining
when a Scientist was fully sharing in a joint decision had
changed. Before the changes described in Chapter II, the

question in the minds of the men was primarily whether the Manager listened to a Scientist's advice and took his opinions into account when the Manager made the decision. Now the question was whether the Scientists' professional knowledge constituted an independent base of authority alongside the positional authority of the Manager. The men had acquired a new standard for defining their own relationships. Using this new standard, more Non-CAPS Junior Scientists classified the decision-making procedure in their groups as ultimately based on positional authority alone. Since this had been the accepted relationship in their departments before, and since the Non-CAPS Junior Scientists had had nothing to cause them to expect otherwise, a large proportion of the Non-CAPS Junior Scientists now stated that this was the relationship they preferred to have. Among the CAPS Junior Scientists, however, whatever changes had taken place had been swallowed up in the redefinition. Some of the CAPS Junior Managers had changed, but the changes which had taken place had been offset by the heightened expectations of the CAPS Junior Scientists. Therefore, in the CAPS departments, even though there had been some gains for the Junior Scientists in influence and autonomy, the gains fell short of expectations and the net effect was an increased dissatisfaction.

Summary

The organizational changes described in Chapter II had had a varied effect on the operations of the Center and on the members of the organization. There had been nothing to suggest a "Hawthorne effect" but neither had the program been ineffectual. Just as the organizational changes themselves had been technical and focused, the outcomes had been specific rather than general, particular rather than universal.

For the Senior Scientists and the Junior Managers in the

experimental (CAPS) departments, the organizational
changes had brought both greater autonomy in the conduct
of their work and increased opportunity to use authority.
Both these groups reported increased productivity and satisfaction. The Senior Managers and Junior Scientists in these
departments experienced a relative reduction in authority.
Their contact with others who made decisions, according to
their reports, had been curtailed; they were now less likely
than before to be present in settings where decisions were
made, and men whom they had influenced before now
listened to others. These two groups were consistently less
positive in their evaluation of effects of the program.

The CAPS Senior Scientists were the most likely of the
four groups to evaluate all the outcomes of the change
affirmatively. They reported finding themselves in less frequent contact with their superiors, exercising greater autonomy in their work and more a part of the decision-making
process at the Center than before. At the end of the 15-month
period, they were more satisfied than any other group with
the organization's capabilities. Three-fourths of them reported an increase in their own productivity, and they were
more likely than any other group to see an improvement in
the functioning of others around them. With the CAPS
Junior Managers, they were most likely to report an increase
in involvement and satisfaction with their work. They had
become more satisfied with their immediate chief, and finally
they were the only group which had grown more likely to
say they would ignore offers from other firms.

The CAPS Junior Managers' experiences were somewhat
different from those of the Senior Scientists, but their reactions were similar. Reportedly, their contact with both
their immediate superiors and subordinates had been reduced, but this was offset by greater contact with Senior
Scientists, outsiders, and higher management. They found
themselves with greater autonomy in the conduct of their

work. These reports about authority and influence were accompanied by positive views of the effects of the change. Although they had been the most critical of the organization's competitive abilities before the changes, they now saw improvement. They felt more productive and more involved in their work. Like the CAPS Senior Scientists who reported to the CAPS Senior Managers, they, too, reported increased satisfaction in working under them. They were, however, not so likely as the CAPS Senior Scientists to see an improvement in their work groups (they were working directly with Junior Scientists), nor did they report so much satisfaction in their work. (Some were frustrated by the absence of positional authority as a basis for power in the CAPS committees.) Finally, while they felt the existing changes had been beneficial to the Center, they were relatively reluctant to see any further changes take place, perhaps seeing not only their own authority but positional authority in general threatened by an extension of the changes.

The Director's attempt to get the CAPS Senior Managers to spend part of their time in technical planning had failed, and they had established no new contacts or power position around that activity. It was also clear that the Senior Managers had been pulled away from their supervisory and liaison functions in their departments in other ways. Their subordinates reported less frequent contact with them and everyone agreed that the CAPS Junior Managers had replaced the CAPS Senior Managers as the working communication link with Research and Sales. Other men in the organization, notably the subordinates of these CAPS Senior Managers, viewed the change as having substantially restricted the autonomy and freedom of these Senior Managers. On most questions, the Senior Managers were less positive in their evaluation of the changes than were the two previous groups discussed. Only one of the four felt more productive than before (although two saw improvement in their group's productivity). They were less likely than others to report increases in involvement and satisfaction in their work. There was a drop in expressed satisfaction with their immediate supervisor (the Director). They had reported very high satisfaction with their chief before the changes and the drop still left a very positive attitude, but not quite so high as before. Finally, the CAPS Senior Managers, as well as their Non-CAPS counterparts, were in close agreement that the changes had gone far enough.

The CAPS Junior Scientists were, perhaps, the most interesting group of the four, and the largest group in the CAPS department. Most of the changes had been aimed ultimately at increasing their productivity and involvement, yet the intended positive effects of the program had been least often achieved in this group. In most cases, contact with immediate supervisors had diminished, as well as the ability to influence them. They had been quite satisfied with the Center's competitive edge before the changes, but this satisfaction had eroded. They were less likely than others in CAPS to report increased personal productivity and even less likely to report gains in their group. Increases in involvement and satisfaction in their work were reported but the increases were smaller than in any other CAPS group. Like the Senior Managers, they were less satisfied with their superiors (the CAPS Junior Managers). But perhaps most significant was the fact that they (and three Non-CAPS Senior Scientists) were the only ones who indicated that they would no longer be inclined to ignore offers from other firms. A closer examination of the responses of this group suggested that their dissatisfaction, where present, arose not only from loss of previous authority and influence but from unfulfilled expectations. Satisfaction had dropped most dramatically among those who were brushed by the changes in authority but had ultimately not participated in them.

Note to Chapter IV

The Assessment of Organizational Performance
at the Nampa Development Center

The difficulties in measuring any change in the performance level of an organizational unit engaged in research or development work are illustrated by the attempts made in this study to find performance measures for the experimental departments or even for the Center as a whole. One by one, a number of possible objective measures of performance were explored: numbers of patents, average number of months required from first research report to first full-scale run in a production plant, new product sales volume, and evaluation by men from other parts of the company. One by one, they had to be rejected.

The number of patents obtained during the year by men at the Center as a comparative measure of productivity had to be discarded early. At the Development Center, patents primarily referred to process patents, i.e., patents to protect the company's proprietary right to a way of producing a given material. Actually, the number of patents obtained by the men at the Center had increased over the average number obtained in the previous three years. But when patents were discussed with the managers and scientists at the Center as a measure of productivity or effectiveness, they were unanimous in their opinion that in the Nampa Center the number of patents had no necessary relationship to importance nor to the amount or quality of the work which had gone into them. Often the number of patents were more a function of the particular stage which the projects were in, or policy decisions about meeting competition or foreign licensing arrangements.

The average number of months to complete a project, a second proposed measure, was found to be largely a function of the size and complexity of the projects undertaken. The percentage of projects completed early or on time could only be considered a valid measure of productivity if there could be some way of assuring that target dates had been set in some uniform way. Unfortunately, there was not.

The Director and others at the Center suggested that perhaps the best outside judgment of the Development Center's effectiveness could be obtained from the users of its products and services — the men working in Sales, Research, and Production. They argued that these men would be in a better position than anyone else to compare performance before and after the change. Consequently, interviews were held with 16 men, representatives from each of these areas. Three-fourths of the users of the Center's services judged that improvement had been made in the Division's ability to develop new products. Almost all were in favor of continuing the CAPS program. The evaluation of these users as an objective measure of effectiveness came under suspicion, however, as soon as the interviews were begun, for it quickly became apparent that the men being interviewd were primarily responding to their own improved communication flow with the men at the Center. They had become active participants in the CAPS program themselves and could by no means qualify as "objective" observers. Instead, their perceptions had to be considered in the same category as those of the participants inside the Center.

Finally, sales of new products were seriously considered. The Department of Commerce publishes annually the total national sales in certain broad market areas. One manager in Sales suggested that any increase or decrease in market share in certain areas over a three-year period might provide a criterion for judging the effectiveness of the program. Therefore, records were sought on the sales of each product for the three-year period following the initiation of the CAPS program. However, at the end of that period, it was unclear how much of the increases shown could be related to the work at the Center. Outside factors, including competitors entering or leaving the market, size of the sales effort, and the like, had had such marked independent effects on the percentages that no one at the Center or elsewhere in the Division was willing to say that increases could be attributed to the effects of the organizational changes at the Development Center. Moreover, the product cycle in this industry is such that the impact of new product development is often not fully reflected in sales even in three years.

A final factor which tended further to invalidate any one or a combination of the above indicators as performance measures at Nampa was the fact that a large part of the Center's effort had been devoted to the Filtron Project for several years before the study began. This often made comparisons meaningless. For example, even though the proportion of division sales arising from new products increased for several years following the introduction of the CAPS program, this could also be explained by the fact that a large part of the Center's efforts had been taken from a large and unsuccessful (in terms of company sales) project and applied to several smaller but more promising projects.

CHAPTER V
Change in Organizations

THE PRECEDING chapter examined the results of an effort to introduce change in an operating organization. This chapter will consider some of the factors determining success or failure in such an effort. The initiation of change in organizations is essentially an episode in influence. Typically, someone in the organization comes to view the organization's relation to the environment in terms which call for different behavior on the part of the organization's members. He then seeks to influence others in the organization to change their behavior. The establishment of new behavior patterns represents an extension of this influence as the impetus for the change increasingly comes to reside within the individuals assuming the new behavior. This phenomenon is commonplace in organizational life, yet our understanding of it lags seriously behind the need for such understanding in a swiftly changing society.

The Nampa case provides a setting in which the most prominent features of this phenomenon can be discerned. The events at the Center are representative of many organizational change attempts in that the initial approach taken was the alteration of the formal organization structure. However, unlike most organizational change efforts, the events were carefully noted and consequent effects recorded and analyzed. Perhaps most importantly, the outcomes were not uniform. Some of the Director's objectives were obtained, others were not. Some individuals were affected, others seemed untouched. The contrast between the Director's successful and unsuccessful attempts to influence, therefore, will be the major analytical tool in examining the features of this change effort.

The primary focus will be on the examination of change at the Nampa Center, but the results of other studies of change will also be introduced to clarify and amplify what is found in this instance.

Comparison of change efforts and their effects in this and other investigations draws attention to two prior conditions characteristic of successful attempts to initiate change. The first is the experiencing of stress by the individuals involved. In both the Nampa situation and the other studies examined, when individuals experienced little stress, the likelihood of actual change was low. The second condition concerns the authority and power of the person initiating the change. Members of an organization respond positively to attempts at influence when they perceive the initiator as a prestigeful and powerful figure. The initiator's power might derive from any of several sources, but most frequently it is multiply-based, including both high position and professional competence.

The successful initiation of change, however, does not assure the continuation and persistence of new behavior patterns. Several features tend to distinguish clearly between those change effects in which new behavior patterns are established and those which fail in this respect. These features can best be described as concurrent movements along four different dimensions:

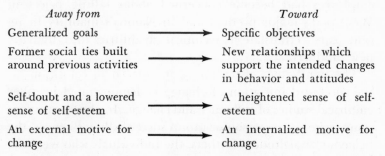

Away from	*Toward*
Generalized goals	Specific objectives
Former social ties built around previous activities	New relationships which support the intended changes in behavior and attitudes
Self-doubt and a lowered sense of self-esteem	A heightened sense of self-esteem
An external motive for change	An internalized motive for change

The remainder of the chapter will be devoted to a closer

examination of these features of organizational change. The two conditions which tend to characterize the successful initiation of change will be considered first, followed by an examination of each of the four dimensions noted above and the progression needed along each to establish new patterns of behavior and thought.

TENSION AS A PRIOR CONDITION

Corporate management's decision to abandon plans to manufacture and market the Filtron units, after most of the technical objectives of the project had been achieved, generated sharp disappointment and frustration among the men at the Nampa Center. For several years a large number of the men had devoted all their efforts to developing the Filtron unit, and though most were willing to acknowledge the probable wisdom of the decision, many had come to identify their future careers with the Filtron Project's success. The picture was further clouded by other recent developments in the Westwood Division's major product line. In its early years, the Division had rapidly developed several highly profitable new products with the Nampa Center playing a key role. At the time this study began, Westwood was still the most profitable division in the company and was considered a leader in its industry, but many of Nampa's employees had become concerned about falling prices in Westwood's major product and in Nampa's inability in recent years to translate its technical capabilities into dramatic new products.

The significance of tension as an antecedent condition for the successful initiation of change is demonstrated in other empirical studies of influence and change. In almost every instance where one person or group successfully influenced the behavior or attitudes of others, the individuals who were the objects of influence experienced a more-than-usual amount of tension or stress prior to the time when influence was exerted.* Guest, in his three-year study of leadership and successful organizational change in an automobile assembly plant, reported great tension in the plant before the new production manager arrived. Labor grievances and turnover were high, the plant had the highest costs and poorest quality record in its division, and received constant pressure from division headquarters. Moreover, the "members of the Plant Y staff were acutely aware of the situation." [1]

Seashore and Bower, in their report of a successful change effort by a consulting-research team noted that in the year prior to the interventions of the team, "Banner [the com-

___

* This uniformity was also evident in a wide variety of non-organizational settings such as rehabilitation groups, psychotherapy, and so-called "thought-reform" prisons where there was a conscious attempt being made to influence behavior and attitudes. These are qualitatively different situations from industrial settings. Alcoholics, Communist prisoners, and psychiatric patients share an emotional distress and lack of control over their own actions which clearly differentiate them from the men at the Nampa Center. But it is worth noting that in these settings, as well, attempts to influence behavior have a high probability of success only when the individuals who are the objects of influence have been experiencing internal stress.

Certain organizations, such as Alcoholics Anonymous, whose central aim is to induce specific behavioral change, refuse to admit anyone unless he is consciously experiencing distress. An applicant to A.A. must openly admit the failure of previous individual efforts and his need for help. (Schein, *Coercive Persuasion*, p. 272.) In psychotherapy, Frank argues that presence of prior emotional distress is related to the results of the treatment:

The importance of emotional distress in the establishment of a fruitful psychotherapeutic relationship is suggested by the facts that the greater the overall degree of expressed distress, as measured by a symptom check list, the more likely the patient is to remain in treatment, while conversely two of the most difficult categories of patients to treat have nothing in common except lack of distress. (Frank, *Persuasion and Healing*, p. 136.)

Even in the so-called thought-reform prisons, where the interrogator had the power to induce new stress, the presence of internal tension prior to imprisonment was a critical factor in the prisoner's susceptibility to influence and attitude change. E. H. Schein and his associates, who studied the Chinese thought-reform program as reported by American civilian prisoners in Chinese prisons, assigned a crucial role to the sense of guilt experienced by the individual. They reported that "if the prisoner-to-be was susceptible to social guilt, he was particularly vulnerable to the pressure of the cellmates in a group cell." (Schein, *op. cit.*, p. 167.)

pany] dropped to a very marginal profit position. . . .
Waste, service, and quality problems arose. . . . There was
a sense of things getting out of control, a feeling shared and
expressed by many non-managerial people." [2]

Elliott Jaques, in his pioneering study of social and technical change in the Glacier Metal Company, reported the
impact of a crisis which resulted in a large number of layoffs and "great anxiety about job security." The procedure
adopted to handle the layoffs had lessened some of the morale
problems, but it did not and could not remove everyone's
anxiety about job security.[3] Jaques, in fact, concluded that a
necessary factor in allowing for working-through of group
problems was a "problem severe and painful enough for its
members to wish to do something about it." [4]

Blake, Mouton, Barnes, and Greiner described a major organizational change effort featuring a training program and
carefully noted the tension in the Sigma plant prior to the
training consultant's arrival at the plant. A merger had taken
place, bringing the plant under a new headquarters staff,
and a serious problem arose over the "use of Sigma manpower on construction work of new projects." When the
headquarters staff began to "prod Sigma," the plant management "became defensive" and, according to one of the managers at headquarters, "some of our later sessions became
emotional." In addition, "strained relations between different departments and levels within the plant began to develop." [5] Greiner reported that "plant morale slipped badly,
insecurity arose, and performance slumped." One of the
managers within the plant said that "everything seemed to
get out of control." [6]

Tension and Coalitional Power

The presence or absence of tension is less important, however, than the *locus* of tension for change in an organization
as methods and outcomes of attempts at change are tied to

the locus. If the tension exists primarily among those at the top of the authority structure, but not among those below, change efforts will be attempted through the existing authority structure. Resistance, if any, will usually be in the form of circumvention and token compliance. If, on the other hand, tension exists only at the bottom of the authority structure, attempts to change the organization may take the form of a revolt and an attack on the existing authority structure, as in the Berkeley campus riots and in wildcat strikes.

The situation at Nampa represents yet a third type, where tension and a desire for change existed at more than one level in the hierarchy, creating a bimodal distribution. The Director felt a strong need for change. New to the position of top executive at the Center and bringing with him new ways of viewing the Center and its task, he saw in the environment, and in the Center's relationship to that environment, a need for internal change as well as an opportunity to prove himself as a manager.

The Senior Managers expressed little dissatisfaction or desire for change. Through demonstrated ability and their arrival at the Center in its formative period, they had risen rapidly to responsible positions relative to their age, thus having a high investment in the system as it stood. Not only had they been able to work relatively well within the existing system, but they had been amply rewarded under it and saw much less need for change.

The Junior Managers, on the other hand, were dissatisfied. On the average only a few years younger than the Senior Managers, they had come to the Center a few years after its opening and had therefore spent most of their time there during a period of relatively slow expansion. A number were eager to demonstrate that they could handle greater responsibility.

The Senior Scientists had come to the Center at about

the same time as the Senior Managers but had not moved into management positions, being assigned, in large part, to staff specialist positions. At the time of that assignment they had been led to expect that through advice and special analysis they could influence the implementation of development projects. Instead, they were repeatedly frustrated by the line groups' failure to allow them to help define the problems.

Finally, the Junior Scientists were a mixed group. Some were well satisfied with their careers and prospects at the Center; some were too new to the Center to have become dissatisfied, while still others were very much concerned about the number of years spent at the Center without promotion or added responsibility.

An implied coalition formed out of the particular distribution of discontent at Nampa. The Director provided the initiation and legitimacy of change, while the CAPS Junior Managers and Senior Scientists supplied support from below. The strength of this coalition lay in the strategic roles played by each of these groups in the new structure and a spiraling effect came into play. The motivation of the Junior Managers and Senior Scientists to support the program increased as a result of expanded authority in their new roles. These gains in authority tended to increase their enthusiasm for the program and their willingness to lend their support.

AUTHORITY AND POWER OF THE INFLUENCER

The forces for change represented by tension and the desire for change must be mobilized, however, and given direction. Those forces acting to resist change in some given direction must be overcome, neutralized, or enlisted. In an organization, unless there is to be protracted resistance, someone must gain the acceptance and possible support of individuals not seeking change and even of those who feel threatened by it. The initiator of change gains support and overcomes resistance in proportion to his power and the relevance of his power to the objectives of the organization. His power in turn stems in large measure from the multiple sources of authority attached to his position in the structure.

In organizational studies of change, successful attempts at change were consistently initiated by the formal head of the organizational unit involved or else given his strong support. The initiator of change in Guest's study was the new plant manager. Moreover, he enjoyed a reputation for success in his previous position, and it became obvious to other employees that he had the support of the district manager and the ability to influence his superiors.[7] Pelz reports on the necessity of upward influence by those not heads of organizations in his study of first line superiors.[8] Similarly, Jaques had the active support of the Managing Director of Glacier Metal.[9]

The changes at the Banner Corporation,[10] were initiated by the Plant Manager, the highest official at the plant. He consulted and gained support from Rensis Likert and others at the University of Michigan, and brought in an agent from the Survey Research Center who carried with him the prestige of a university member as well as the authority of an experienced manager. In another study the Plant Manager and the consultant, Dr. Blake, who "had an impressive reputation with management in other parts of the [headquarters company]," both strongly advocated the change program at the Sigma plant.[11]

Non-organizational settings show the same link between prestige and influence: individuals tend to believe and do those things suggested by authoritative, prestigeful sources.[12] Goal-setting studies reported by Mace indicate that setting goals for individuals and implicitly associating these goals with prestigeful authorities using terms such as "scientific progress" or "the advancement of research" have a favorable effect on performance.[13] Studies of operant conditioning of verbal behavior found that when the persuader has some prestige or power in the subject's eyes, the influence is stronger and more consistent. Students are more consistently influenced by their instructors, for example, than by fellow students.*

This feature of the change process was demonstrated by its presence, but not by its absence, in the Nampa situation. A part of the new Director's task was to establish confidence in the men at the Center that the changes could actually be effected as proposed. Initially, their willingness to believe that the changes would produce results beneficial to them had to come largely from their confidence in his position and personal judgment.

The Director started from a position of relative strength. He had recently been made chief executive at the Center and, on paper at least, had the authority to direct whatever changes in the structure and operations of the Center he

---

* Another area of study in which the persuasive influence of a prestigeful figure in whom the subject places confidence and trust is concerned with faith-healing and the so-called "placebo effect" in medicine. Frank reports that even healers regarded by the community as charlatans or quacks were able to bring symptom relief to persons who regarded them as sources of authority and power. Their success appeared to rest on their ability to evoke the patient's expectancy of help. In medical treatment the fact that relief and healing can be brought about solely by the patient's expectation of help from the physician is demonstrated by experiments verifying the so-called "placebo effect." In these studies, the doctor administers a pharmacologically inert substance to the patient rather than an active medication. Since the placebo is inert, its beneficial effects derive from the patient's confidence in the doctor's prescription and in the institutions of science and medicine which he represents. There is evidence that placebos can have marked physiological effects. Studies have shown that their use has been accompanied by healing of tissue damage ranging from warts to peptic ulcers. A similar effect is the "hello-goodbye" effect in psychotherapy. Patients who merely had contact with a prestigeful (in their eyes) psychiatrist improved significantly over the individuals in a control group who were placed on a waiting list and did not see a psychiatrist. In fact, these minimal contact patients showed almost as much improvement of certain kinds as a third group who underwent prolonged treatment. (Frank, *op. cit.*, pp. 60–61 and 65–74.)

deemed necessary. The only man in senior management at the Development Center with a Ph.D., he had an enviable record of technical achievements, his work having resulted in a large number of patents. His promotions had been rapid and those who had worked for him described him as very capable and a "real gentleman" who was "genuinely concerned about others." Thus, the Director's authority was drawn from all three of the sources described in Chapter III: (1) on the authority based on the position he now held, (2) on his expertise in conducting and directing technical work, and (3) on his own personal characteristics and reputation.

On the other hand, he was new to this position and untested in managing a large organization. With some of the men his relationships had recently been those of a peer rather than a superior. Moreover, although the chief executive at the Center, he was subordinate to others in the company management structure and his actions were subject to their review. Since the Director was proposing a course of action not followed by his predecessors, his subordinates were keeping an eye on the reactions of those above him.

The Director, therefore, increased his power by building on the authority he already possessed. He first reached upward in the organization to gain demonstrable support for his program and could show that he had the active collaboration of the corporate Vice President of Research and Development and the divisional Vice President of Marketing by having their subordinates in research and sales assigned to work on the CAPS committees. Perhaps more significantly, the divisional Vice President of Development, to whom the Director reported, participated in the Caps committee reviews every three weeks. The Director's "authority of knowledge" — his image as someone with significant ideas about the management of technical development — gained subtle support through having a team of university investigators devote time and money to study his new program.

Finally, through his own enthusiasm and conviction the
Director elicited important support based on the personal
loyalties and high personal regard for him in the Center.

There is, of course, abundant evidence in our own study
and elsewhere to deny that any change initiated by a powerful source will be successful. Behavioral change is more complex than that. But the initiator's power seems to be a necessary, if not sufficient, condition for introducing large scale
change in an organizational system. Where a person planning to initiate change does not already possess power in
the organization, it is his first task to develop "social capital"
for himself, i.e., to build up his power in the social system he
intends to change.[14]

Movement Toward Increasingly Specific Objectives

A sustained movement from generalized toward specific
objectives was the first consistent pattern noted in instances
where new behavior patterns were established. As the new
programs gained momentum, in the Nampa Center, for
example, the targets for the Junior Managers and Senior
Scientists in the CAPS departments steadily assumed greater
immediacy and concreteness. For the Senior Managers and
Junior Scientists, however, objectives remained general and
somewhat diffuse.

The changes outlined for the Junior Managers began,
but did not remain, at a very general level. Junior Managers
were told they were to take over more responsibility in managing their own groups. Not long afterward they were asked
to prepare a budget request for their groups for the coming
year, an activity previously handled by the Senior Managers.
At the beginning the Junior Managers were to have the
responsibility of "planning the technical work" for their
groups and of setting up a timetable for the completion of
the various phases of their projects, a relatively general ob-

jective. With the coming of the CAPS committees, they were given specific responsibility for producing one new product or product modification and a target date for having it ready for transfer to production. They were asked to divide the overall task into smaller units and work out a week-by-week projected schedule for completion of the various subunits of the task, and they were held responsible for monitoring their own schedules. If a CAPS group lagged behind schedule, the Junior Manager was expected to recommend the allocation of more men and money or the revision of the work schedule.

Similarly, the Senior Scientists' original assignment to "find some way to make themselves more useful to the line groups" was general and lacked concreteness. But with the formation of the CAPS committees, they were assigned to particular projects. They attended planning meetings and participated in the formulation and monitoring of the detailed time schedules. Moreover, they assumed responsibility for obtaining and coordinating other staff services needed by their particular project.

Neither the CAPS Senior Managers nor the CAPS Junior Scientists moved from the general to the specific. The Senior Managers' assignment to spend half their time doing long-range technical planning remained essentially at that level of generality, as neither the Director nor the Senior Managers worked out intermediate or sub-objectives. The absence of a movement toward specificity is not quite so clear in the case of the Junior Scientists, but the pattern is similar. An overall objective that the Junior Scientists should be given more responsibility and become more deeply involved in carrying out tasks was announced at the beginning of the period under study. But no concrete sub-objectives were established as a means of reaching this end. In some of the groups the Junior Managers did work out with their men ways in which this general objective could be made operational, and in these instances Junior Scientists came to the meetings, made reports, and took over all responsibility for parts of the project. In many of the groups, however, CAPS Junior Scientists reported that their daily activities had been essentially unaffected by the change.

The same phenomenon appeared in the other studies examined. In each instance where someone successfully influenced another person or group of persons to change their behavior or attitudes, the movement toward greater specificity of goals and objectives was one of the common features of the process. Sometimes the initiator of change sets the sub-goals and sometimes those being influenced set them, often it was a joint or an alternating arrangement. But the consistent element is that someone sets concrete sub-goals. Guest reported that the new manager at Plant Y, for example, began by outlining a "few general goals" such as better planning. He set up meetings for discussing general problems, but attention was steadily brought to focus on improving specific areas such as accounting methods and inspection procedures.[15]

Jaques' report of a three-year period of change in the Glacier Metal Company described how a project team worked successfully with councils and management groups at various levels and departments throughout the organization. The process followed by the team in its work with each group showed remarkable consistency, beginning with the general goal of "understanding their difficulties," moving to a goal of understanding their own "here-and-now" relationships, and finally heading toward the resolution of specific problems or the writing of a new constitution.[16]

The Plant Manager's initially announced objective at Banner Corporation was to introduce "participative management" into the organization. After several months, four sub-goals were established for implementing the overall goal:

(1) increased emphasis on the work group as a functioning unit,

(2) more supportive behavior from supervisors,

(3) greater employee participation in decision making, and

(4) increased interaction and influence among work group members.

A series of meetings with all the supervisors in the experimental department then followed in which the objective became more and more operational in the minds of the supervisors. Finally, these intermediate goals were translated into more specific goals such as bringing the employees into the decisions about a new shift rotation scheme.[17]

The changes reported by Blake, Mouton, Barnes, and Greiner at the Sigma plant followed an identical pattern,[18] beginning with a training program in which the objectives, for the participants, were their own style of managing. Other meetings of work groups followed in which the objectives were to explore ways to transfer "the general concepts and personal learning of the Seminars" to the operation of their own group. The objective became even more concrete as the men consciously tried to use some of their new problem-solving methods in working out a program for reducing utility costs and in a difficult union-management contract negotiation.*

---

* Outside the organizational setting, perhaps the most carefully conceptualized example of this aspect of the change process is found in the descriptions of the therapeutic process. Early in the relationship between the patient and the therapist, the mutually understood objective is usually relatively general in character: to enable the patient to operate more effectively in his environment, to find relief from serious distress, or to achieve an understanding of the patient's problems and their causes. Explorations may begin by looking at the patient's past behavior, his relationships outside therapy, and his feelings about these. But most schools of therapy agree that as the relationship continues, the patient comes to show feelings and behavior toward the therapist similar to those making trouble for him outside therapy. The examination of these concrete specific events acted out in their own relationship is undertaken as a means of achieving the more general objective. (Stein, ed., *Contemporary Psychotherapies.*)

Altering Old Relationships and Establishing New Ties

Loosening prior social ties and establishing new relationships which supported the intended changes in attitude and behavior was the second pattern characterizing successful change at the Center. The old behavior and attitudes were deeply imbedded in relationships built up over the years, and as long as the individuals involved maintained these relationships unaltered, changes were both difficult and transitory. New behavior patterns were most readily and firmly established when they were conditions of regular membership in a new group.

At Nampa the only men who did not move along this dimension were those in the Non-CAPS groups. Their old relationships remained almost intact, and despite the changes taking place around them, they changed their behavior or attitude very little. On the other hand, almost all the men in the CAPS departments reported some change in their former relationships. The Director's organizational innovations had the effect, either intentionally or unintentionally, of loosening significant interpersonal ties for the men in each of the four CAPS categories. Changes in job requirements removed the activities around which some relationships had been built, and alterations in work schedules and locations broke up other former important interaction patterns. As shown earlier, the men in each CAPS group reported a decrease in contact with either their immediate superior or their immediate subordinates. [Chapter IV, Figure 6]

The important tie between the Senior and Junior Managers was purposely loosened. The new duties and the meetings the CAPS committees created absorbed much of the Junior Managers' time and attention. In addition, the Junior Managers and Senior Managers were not the valuable source of aid to each other which they had been before. The Senior Managers were no longer the exclusive communication link or the only source of direction for the Junior Managers with higher management and with Research and Sales. Neither were the Junior Managers the ready source of assistance to the Senior Managers in performing overall departmental tasks which they had been before. Along this dimension, the experience of the Senior Scientists paralleled that of the Junior Managers.

Although this same result had not been anticipated between the Junior Managers and the Junior Scientists who worked under them, contact also became less frequent in this relationship through the time and attention which the Junior Managers devoted to the CAPS committees.

The differences among the four groups along this dimension, then, were not in the alteration of old relationships, but rather in the extent to which new social relationships were established which would support the new ways of behaving and thinking. The organizational changes the Director introduced brought both the Junior Managers and the Senior Scientists into new patterns of interaction and social exchange in which the social pressure was to adhere to the new role definition and abandon the old. For example, when the CAPS committee made a joint decision, and the Junior Managers and the Senior Scientists sitting in the committee agreed to a particular way of implementing that decision, there was strong social pressure on these men to resist attempts by their own superiors (Senior Managers) to get them to do something else first or to perform the work in a different way. Of course, the influence of the Senior Manager was still strong, but a change had occurred. The relationship with the Senior Manager no longer had the potency it once had, and the other members of the CAPS committee acted as a new reference group supporting the altered behavior and attitudes. Even the new relationship directly between the Junior Managers and the Senior Scientists had this effect, cementing each other into the new roles they were now beginning to play. The Senior Managers and Junior Scientists did not establish any new relationships. Their previous ties were attenuated, but they formed no new relationships which might have pulled them more deeply into new patterns of activities and beliefs.

In other studies of change, it is this dimension of the change phenomenon which has been most explicitly recognized: the beliefs, attitudes, and activities of a person are closely related to his reference groups.[19] Certainly not all of an individual's former associations will counteract an intended change, nor will new groups formed in a change situation always work in the direction which the influencing agent intends, but in general any significant changes in activities or attitudes include some movement from old object relationships toward new ones.

Behavioral scientists did not originate the idea that an alteration of old relationships facilitates change in individuals or groups. Most influencing institutions in our society separate the individual whom they wish to influence from his regular social contacts and routines. Convents, monasteries, and prisons tend to make this a total separation, and educational institutions make the separation to a lesser degree by their physical distance from home and a demanding work load.* The individual's greater susceptibility to influence when he is separated from social contacts which support his current beliefs was ingeniously demonstrated by the famous Asch experiments: when subjects were placed in a situation where no other person agreed with the subject's own judgments, a third of the subjects came to doubt their own perceptions to the extent that they reported seeing

---

* Perhaps the best reported study of this is the work done by Newcomb at Bennington College. During their four years at the college, the girls increasingly took on the attitudes of the faculty and student leaders and relinquished those of their parents. See Newcomb, "Attitude Development as a Function of Reference Groups." See also Schein and Bennis, *Personal and Organizational Change Through Group Methods,* pp. 270–271.

what the others reported in over half the trials. Yet, if only one person in the group confirmed a subject's own perceptions, his resistance to social pressure was significantly increased.[20]

Rice, in his study of change in a textile weaving mill in India, found some confirmation for his argument that this need for removal from previous contacts applied also to groups where the group was the focus of change, as otherwise the prior social relationships would continue to support the behavior patterns and attitudes which the change program was trying to alter.[21]

Breaking up or attenuating former social ties may unfreeze an individual or group, but this alone provides no assurance that any resulting changes will be in a given direction or that the unfreezing will have any permanency, as was seen in the Nampa case. Formation of new relationships which reward and support the desired behaviors and confirm the modified attitudes appears to be essential, or there will be a strong pull to return to former activities and attitudes and to the relationships which supported and reinforced them.

An interesting study illustrating this phenomenon was a follow-up study of the effects of an International Harvester Company training program, emphasizing "human relations" skills which were categorized by the investigators as consideration. Tested before and after the two-week training program, the foremen's attitude test scores initially showed an increase on consideration, but over time the scores shifted until these foremen actually scored lower on consideration than a control group which had not been trained. Only those foremen whose immediate superiors scored high on consideration continued to score high themselves. The other foremen, whose superiors did not place a high value on consideration, returned to a pattern very close to that of their chief. Daily interaction negated the effects of the training program. The foremen's prior ties were interrupted during the two-week training period, but the men then returned to a situation where the most significant and relevant relationship was with their own supervisors. No continuing new relationships had been established which could act to confirm and reinforce any attitude changes begun during the training program.[22]

A study differing in important ways from the International Harvester study, yet confirming its findings, is Barnes and Greiner's investigation of the effects of Blake's organization development program at the Sigma plant. At Sigma the management and staff members at all levels of the plant went through an initial training program during which men were removed from their regular work groups and placed among relative strangers. They then returned to their old work groups, as in the International Harvester program, but with the difference that their superiors and colleagues had also been through the same training experience. A second series of meetings involved immediate superiors and subordinates. These teams examined their own managerial practices and set up specific goals for change.

A follow-up study revealed that the program had had an impact on the plant's operations and on the behavior and attitudes of some of the men, but again, not all. Those managers who were viewed as "most improved" by their subordinates tended to have superiors (in 77% of the cases) and a majority of colleagues (in 92% of the cases) who were also seen among the "most improved." In contrast, "least improved" managers had "most improved" bosses in only 55% of the cases and a majority of "most improved" colleagues in only 26% of the cases. Strong support from superiors and colleagues apparently accompanied, and may even have been necessary for, individual change among the managers. In fact, it appeared to the investigators that even the presence of only one "least improved" cynic was enough to have a strong dampening effect, since 60% of the "most improved" supervisors worked in settings where there were no "least improved" colleagues whatsoever.[23] Thus, as in the Nampa and International Harvester studies, there was no behavioral change unless the relationships changed to support the new behavior. The Sigma study differs from the Nampa case in one significant way: the major reinforcing relationships in the Sigma study were among the same people as before the change. The parties to the relationship had not changed, but the relationships had. This, of course, has important implications for an administrator who wishes to maintain his work teams intact, but to alter behavior and attitudes in these groups. But the point to be made here is that unless the relationships change, behavioral change is difficult. Whether or not changed relationships can be most effectively accomplished when there are actually new members introduced is not the issue here.

Guest's study of successful change in the automobile assembly plant reported high incidence of personnel shifts breaking up old social ties on a large scale and establishing new relationships supporting the new behavior patterns. There were few discharges, but a program of planned and deliberate lateral transfers and promotions was instituted. Only 25% of the plant's supervisors held the same job throughout the period studied. Moreover, the Plant Manager set up a new pattern of interactions through an increased use of meetings.

> The scope and function of the meetings established by the new manager stood in marked contrast to those of the earlier period: there were more of them, they were regularly scheduled, they covered a wider range of activities, more people took part in them. . . .[24]

The relationships built up in these meetings were established around a new set of attitudes and behaviors, with support and reinforcement for the new behavior patterns coming from these new ties. On the other hand, the studies reported by Jaques and by Seashore and Bower focused on changes in the nature of the existing relationships. Jaques found that at Glacier Metal a number of new relationships were established around the new activities (new worker-management committees and the like), but the primary thrust of the research team's efforts was to alter the expectations and the reinforcement patterns in the existing relationships, primarily through what they termed "role clarification" and "working through." Role clarification consisted of a joint examination of the several roles members were expected to play in the group and in the organization, as well as the achievement of a common set of expectations about the new ways in which these roles were to be filled. Jaques described "working through" as a serious attempt to voice the unrecognized difficulties, often socially taboo, which had been preventing the group from going ahead with whatever task it may have had. The research team did not focus on "working through" to aid in the solution of any one problem but rather to alter the relationship and the manner of working together, acting on the thesis that, "Once a group has developed insight and skill in recognizing forces related to status, prestige, security . . . these forces no longer colour subsequent discussion nor impede progress to the same extent as before" (p. 307).*

---

* Outside organizational settings, the most vivid example of the new social interactions acting to bring about the intended change itself is found in the reports of the "struggle sessions" in thought-reform prisons. In some reform prisons on the Chinese mainland, western prisoners were placed in cells with a group of "advanced" prisoners, who had already made confessions or were in the process of making them. These prisoners, who themselves were taking on the reformed attitudes and who were given to understand that the progress of the entire cell depended on the performance of the least-reformed member, exerted strong pressures (accusations, browbeating) on their new member. The potency of this pressure from fellow prisoners was so pronounced that Schein concluded it was the single most effective device used to influence the prisoners to confess and change attitudes. (Schein, *op.*

Explanations which lay complete stress on group membership and social pressure for understanding the change process are incomplete, but movement along this dimension appears to be necessary for establishing significant and lasting
behavioral change.

HEIGHTENING SELF-ESTEEM

Increasing self-esteem also appears to be an integral part
of the phenomenon of behavioral and attitudinal change.
Interestingly, moving toward greater self-esteem seems to be
a facilitating factor not only in establishing new patterns of
thought and action, but also in unfreezing old patterns. Aban-
doning previous patterns of behavior and thought is less difficult when an individual is moving toward an increased sense of
his own worth. Movement along this continuum is away from
a sense of self-doubt toward a feeling of positive worth, from

---

cit., p. 193). The Communist prison struggle groups are an extreme form of
a group influencing a new member to assume new behaviors and attitudes,
but the same process goes on in all groups with lowered intensity. The
entering member in almost any group is required to demonstrate adherence
to the norms and values of the group to a greater extent, even, than established members in order to gain full acceptance. (See Homans, *The Human
Group*.)

The establishment of new social ties for confirmation and reinforcement
of changes already begun has also traditionally been a part of evangelistic
programs. John Wesley organized his converts into small units of twelve or
less. This small group, with a chosen leader, met together weekly to tell of
their experiences. The leader visited a member each week to collect dues
and to verify the sincerity of his conversion. Quarterly, each member was
reissued a ticket of membership admitting him to sacrament meetings. Back-
sliding was watched carefully and even three or four absences could bring
the loss of his ticket and expulsion from the Society. (Sargent, *Battle for the
Mind*.) The importance of the establishment of new social relationships
which confirm and support change begun is probably best illustrated by
examining change attempts where old social relationships do not change and
new ties are not established. Following a recent Billy Graham crusade in
New York City, an informal survey of individuals who came forward and
were converted during the crusade found that only those who were subse-
quently integrated into local churches maintained their faith. For others, the
conversion became merely a temporary and lapsed response. (Schein, *op.
cit.*, p. 282.)

a feeling of partial inadequacy toward a confirmed sense of personal capacity. The increased sense of one's own potential is evident all along this continuum, not merely at the end.

The Director's meeting with the Junior Managers in which he announced the first phase of the new program illustrates the means by which this phenomenon is set into motion. The Director outlined the problems he saw and noted where the Center had not been realizing its potential. He spelled out some of the opportunities which had been missed and the potential which was not being realized. While offering no explicit words of approbation or praise to the Junior Managers, he made it clear that he was making an investment in them. He focused his attention on them and on the tasks they were to perform, signaling by his assignment his faith in their capacity to change and take on more responsibility. They were to be the central figures in a new experiment, its success depending largely on them, but they would have to change their behavior to make it successful.

As noted earlier, one of the precursors to successful change is the experience of stress within the system. Though stress is usually found before the intervention of the change agent, the influencing agent himself can play an extremely important role in challenging the individual's sense of adequacy.* As happened in the Nampa case,[25] the new executive may confront the organization members with the inconsistency and inefficiency in their operations. An

---

* This negative diagnosis may be either explicit or implicit, as is illustrated in some of our non-organizational settings. The negative diagnosis may be openly stated as when the religious revivalist points to the prospective proselyte's indulgent life and calls him to repentance. The older members at an A.A. meeting may confront the alcoholic with the fact that he is destroying himself and his family. The Communist prison interrogator may insist on the prisoner's "criminal acts against the People." On the other hand, the negative diagnosis may be communicated implicitly by the agent's acting to introduce change such as a psychotherapist embarking on a program of treatment after he has had exploratory talks with the patient.

outside consultant will more often attempt to induce
the confrontation among the members of the client organization. For example, Robert Blake, working with the Sigma
plant, suggested an initial meeting between plant managers
and the headquarters staff at which the problems uncovered
"shocked" the plant management. From this meeting came
the impetus to design a development program in which
each of the members of the supervisory group was likewise
confronted by others' perceptions of his behavior.[26] Jaques
and the research team at Glacier Metal worked with the
staff in their meetings, and through their interpretations
helped them to "express feelings which they had been sup-
pressing sometimes for years." Many, for the first time, were
confronted with the consequences of some of their behavior.[27]

On the other hand, Cooley, the manager of the automobile
assembly plant studied by Guest, entered into a situation
where the men had already had abundant evidence of the
unsatisfactory consequences of their behavior. He only felt
it necessary to acknowledge this evidence.

> In the first meeting with all supervision he put forward what
> he called "a few basic goals" for the organization in terms of
> expected efficiency and quality. He stated candidly to the
> group that Plant Y had a bad reputation. He said he had
> heard that many members of the group were not capable of
> doing their jobs. He said he was "willing to prove that this
> was not so, and until shown otherwise, I personally will have
> confidence in the group." [28]

In each of these instances, the manager or consultant was
signaling that the men needed to change, that their former
performance was not quite adequate or appropriate.

How, then, do these events begin to foster a heightened
sense of worth? The men cannot help feeling that they are
of some worth if they are receiving this much attention and
respect from someone whom they consider important. He is

making an investment in them. In the Nampa case, though communicating a negative evaluation of their present behavior or attitudes, the Director was also signaling that he had higher expectations, saying, in effect, that he respected the potential of those he was trying to change. Moreover, when he communicated his negative diagnosis, he offered hope, implying that there was a better way, and that he knew that better way. The effect on self-esteem is negative in that the attention the men receive derives from their past inadequacy. But in laying a foundation for a new beginning, departing from old patterns, and promising better results in the future, it is positive.

In instances of successful change, there is a movement over time toward increased self-regard as the person finds himself capable of making the changes in behavior or attitude. He experiences a sense of accomplishment, a relief from tension, and a reintegration around a new pattern of activity and thought. The Junior Managers at Nampa had the opportunity to assume new roles and take on new tasks. As they accomplished these tasks, many of which had previously been performed by their immediate superiors, they gained a basis for new confidence rooted in their own achievements. At the same time, through the CAPS committees, the Junior Managers became the outside sources of contact for the Center on their own projects. Finally, they found themselves in regular contact with the Vice President and other top management officials through the reporting meetings. These factors tended to raise their position within their own groups and provided an additional source for esteem-building.

When the CAPS project groups were formed, the staff specialists, who constituted most of the Senior Scientists involved in the organizational change, were assigned to work with specific projects. They had been asked to work with particular groups several times before, but they now were involved in the actual details of the problems. This time they found the Junior Managers were depending on them to decide what kind of analytical work was needed. Moreover, the Senior Scientists were now assuming part of the senior advisor role, previously the sole province of the Senior Managers. The relationship between the Senior Scientists and the Junior Managers was different in an important way from that between the Senior Managers and Junior Managers, of course: the Junior Managers were not subordinates of the Senior Scientists. But the opportunity to provide experienced counsel and to arrange for valuable technical assistance was now open to the Senior Scientists as it never had been before. This was true partly because the Senior Scientists were assigned to specific CAPS projects with a Junior Manager but, perhaps more importantly, because the partial removal of the Senior Managers from the details of the technical work created a vacuum into which the Senior Scientists were pulled. The Junior Managers still had need of such counsel and help, and in helping to fill this need, the Senior Scientists found a rich source for building self-esteem.

What opportunities for esteem-building were available to the other two groups whom the Director hoped to influence? A number of decision-making responsibilities formerly held solely or jointly by the Senior Managers had now passed to the Junior Managers. The CAPS committee meetings, from which the Senior Managers were excluded, became the setting in which many decisions were made as well as the point of contact with representatives from Research and Sales. Thus the Senior Managers lost both the function and status which had been theirs as the outside contact men for the groups in their departments. Senior Scientists replaced Senior Managers as advisors and contact men in arranging for technical services. Finally, frequent meetings in which the Junior Managers reported project status directly to the Director and Vice President reduced the role of the Senior Managers in the vertical communication chain.

To counteract the loss of these sources of esteem, the Director told the Senior Managers that they were to spend a substantial portion of their time in long-range planning for the Center and the Division. Persons assigned to this activity sometimes deal with broad issues which can be of vital concern to the organization, but the activity is also isolated from current and immediate decisions, and executives are sometimes "kicked upstairs" to long-range planning to remove them from positions where they can make important current decisions. It can be a sign of genuine recognition, but it has also been used as a disguised method of "relieving" a person of a responsible position. The ambiguity of the status of this assignment, as well as the absence of structural mechanisms to give it specificity, combined to make it an unpromising source of esteem-gratification. During the period of the study, the Senior Managers did not fulfill this part of their assignment. They had many current and immediate demands on their time, and it is impossible to determine what effect the ambiguous nature of the activity itself had in influencing their decisions to meet the other demands instead of the Director's injunction to do long-range planning.

The Junior Scientists experienced no loss in sources of esteem, but neither were there any specific changes built into the Director's program to provide an opportunity for them to build esteem. The Director had expressed the hope that the Junior Scientists might share in the increased responsibility given to the Junior Managers — that the Junior Managers, who had been given many new responsibilities, would turn over more of their duties to the men under them. The data indicate that although this happened in some of the project groups, there were many groups in which it did not. Where the Junior Scientists were allowed an increased share in the planning and decision making, the conditions facilitating at least this part of the change process were present. But in the many groups where it did not develop spontaneously, nothing had changed to provide for an increase in self-esteem among the Junior Scientists.

The movement toward greater self-esteem is evident in each of the other four change studies used here to compare with the Nampa case. Early in each of the studies, managers began listening to their subordinates and responding to them. In each of these organizations, subordinates took on responsibilities and participated in decisions withheld from them in the past, and the confidence gained from success in some of these early attempts led to further steps.

In Guest's study the men expressed an increasing feeling of competence ("Just gradually we learned how to do the job") and confidence in their future ("The foreman knows that if he's got the stuff, he's going to be recognized and promoted"). Toward the end of the period studied by Guest the "promotion" theme was mentioned often in the interviews, whereas three years earlier none had expressed the hope of advancing.[29] At the Sigma plant a new set of programs for increasing productivity and improving costs was confidently and successfully carried out.[30] At Glacier, Jaques reported increased confidence and self-esteem were demonstrated in a capacity to tackle formerly taboo problems with considerably less anxiety.

The study of the Banner Corporation is perhaps the most interesting of the four in that the managers and consultants at Banner were more explicitly aware of the need for a movement toward increased self-esteem in the change process than were the designers of any of the other four change attempts. The consultants initially stated a goal of building "supportive supervisory behavior" which they defined as increasing "the extent to which subordinates (at all levels) experienced positive, ego-sustaining relations with superiors and peers whenever they undertook to act in ways which would promote their common goals." [31] Paradoxically, it was at Banner where increased confidence was most difficult to attain, as the early attempts at supervisory support became the focus of misunderstanding and ill will. The supervisors attempted in good faith to be "supportive" but often found no way to link this up to effort and accomplishment. Undiscriminating and erratic support not only failed to build self-esteem but often tended to undermine it. This factor, plus a deteriorating economic situation and some formal organizational blocks controlled by higher management, tended to retard progress to the point where the agent from the Survey Research Center proposed a suspension of the field work. It was only after a reorganization took place, allowing the plant greater freedom, that the latent gains from the early change efforts began to produce the spiraling of achievement and confidence which increased plant productivity.

Perhaps the best-known demonstration that a heightening of self-worth is an integral part of the influence process comes from an early industrial study, the now-famous Relay Assembly Test Room Experiments begun in 1924 by the Western Electric Company at their Hawthorne works. The tests were initially designed to examine the "relation of quality and quantity of illumination to efficiency in industry," but the baffled experimenters found that productivity increased in their "test groups" and "control groups" in almost equal magnitude. They were getting greater efficiency, but it apparently was not "illumination which was making the difference!" Further study, experimentally varying rest pauses and working hours, again revealed no simple correlation between the experimentally imposed changes and rate of output. Production rose steadily even when the experimental conditions were returned to their original condition.

This time, however, the experimenters took careful note of other factors introduced, one of which was the influence of the experimenters on the girls to increase productivity. Ostensibly, the experiment had not been an attempt to change behavior, and the experimenters disclaimed any conscious desire to influence the girls to increase production. The superintendent's notes concerning the first meeting held with the girls indicated that great care was taken to convince them that the purpose of the test was not to boost production:

> The groups were assured that the test was not being set up to determine the maximum output, and they were asked to work along at a comfortable pace and particularly not to attempt to see how much they could possibly do.[32]

But in fact, the girls received a number of signals which conveyed exactly the opposite message.[33] The superintendent told them that:

> If increased output resulted from better or more satisfactory working conditions, both parties would be the gainers.[34]

Increased productivity *was* what interested the experimenters. The girls could see that it was the production output which was recorded so meticulously and subjected to such careful scrutiny.*

In retrospect, the way the girls were treated appears almost perfectly designed to increase their sense of self-esteem. A new supervisor, the department chief, who was also the test observer, came in at the beginning of the tests and operated much differently from his predecessor. The department chief and the experimenters made every effort to gain the girls' whole-hearted cooperation for each change, consulting them

---

* There seems little doubt that the girls received this message whether the experimenters were consciously trying to convey it or not. Studies have shown that even when one person in a close interpersonal relationship is trying to be "nondirective," the other person's behavior can be strongly influenced by the subtle signals of approval and disapproval which the first person unintentionally gives. (Murray, "A Content Analysis Method for Studying Psychotherapy," p. 420.)

about proposed changes and canceling some changes which did not meet their approval. The girls' health, well-being, and opinions were the subject of great and genuine concern. Investigators spent full time recording and analyzing the girls' output, and the girls were regularly visited by the Superintendent of the Inspection Branch as well as by an intermittent stream of industrial psychologists and university professors. With all this attention, each girl became a valued member of a cohesive and cooperative group, and as their efficiency increased, so did their sense of competence.

The experimenters had sought to hold all factors constant except those they were explicitly manipulating in each period, but in their attempts to provide an optimal climate for objective research, the factors which changed most were the very ones most likely to facilitate change. Each of the conditions and processes so far described was present: (1) the girls, in a new and unfamiliar situation, were tense and unsure; (2) a person holding great prestige in the eyes of the girls introduced the changes; (3) at the beginning the objective which the initiator and the rest of the researchers sought was vague and unclear to the girls, but in reading the reports of the experiments it is clear that to the girls the research had a specific objective — to find ways to increase productivity; (4) the girls were separated from their former associates and formed new ties around new activities and attitudes; (5) finally, the experimenters created conditions which fostered among the girls an increased sense of importance and worth.

The Relay Assembly Test Room Experiments series have been cited by a large number of writers to illustrate a wide variety of phenomena, but what ever else it demonstrates, it provides us with a carefully reported instance of influence and induced change with a movement toward greater self-esteem as an integral part of that process.

INTERNALIZATION

Moving from externalization toward internalization of the change motive is the fourth dimension of change. The motivating force toward a particular change originates outside the individuals to be influenced. Those involved may be actively searching for more adequate behavior and seeking new direction, but the actual type or direction of change originates outside. An influencing agent introduces the plan, the scheme, the interpretation, the suggestion, the idea. Where new behavior patterns are established, however, the individuals involved internalize or come to "own" the rationale for the change.

As an individual accepts influence because the new ideas and the prescribed actions are intrinsically rewarding in coping with external and internal stresses, the change is internalized. He adopts the new behavior because it can be useful in problem solving or because it is congenial to his own orientation.*

In the Nampa Center, as well as in the historical and experimental settings mentioned earlier, internalization consisted of each of three elements: (1) provisions of a new cognitive structure; (2) application and improvisation; (3) verification through experience.

---

* We are very close here to Kelman's formulation of identification. (See "Processes of Opinion Change," and "Compliance, Identification and Internalization, Through Processes of Attitude Change.") Kelman, however, argues that internalization is not a necessary part of the influence process. An individual, he reasons, may adopt a new behavior pattern through compliance, not because he believes in the content, but in order to gain a specific reward or to avoid some anticipated punishment. Or he may, through identification, accept influence in order to establish or maintain a relationship with another person or group. This distinction between compliance, identification, and internalization can be made conceptually, but in complex interpersonal relations, in which social influence is being exerted over an extended period of time, neither compliance to external demands nor identification with new reference groups appears to operate successfully without internalization of content on the part of those being influenced. Certainly in the Nampa situation, it would be difficult to explain the changes we have noted in terms of compliance or identification alone.

Provision of a New Cognitive Structure

To judge from the studies examined, the first step in internalization is the influencing agent's introduction of a new conceptual framework. The new framework may be restricted to a way of conceiving a limited set of phenomena, or it may be far-reaching in trying to explain the totality of a person's experience. In either case, the individual is given a new means for reordering information about himself and his environment. Implicit in the framework are relationships of acts to outcomes so that certain ends call for certain behavior. Finally, the influencing agent provides a language which not only communicates the cognitive structure, but creates an "associative net" by which the individual can relate the events in his own life to the new framework.[35]

The Director at Nampa, for example, when first introducing the program, presented his men with a new cognitive structure for interpreting their experience at the Center. He emphasized technical expertise and knowledge of the problem as sources of authority, placing a premium on upward and lateral influence. He questioned the appropriateness of a fixed pyramidal form of organization for the Center's task and proposed a continually reforming organization structure to solve specific problems. Finally, he attempted to replace the number of subordinates as the primary indicator of career progression at the Center with other indicators centering on the complexity and importance of the problem to which a man was assigned.

In each of the other studies of organizational change the person seeking to exert influence provided a new cognitive structure. At the Banner Corporation, for example, the Plant Manager and the consultants agreed that the first step was to "provide the plant management group of fourteen people with a thorough grounding in the concepts and research basis for participation management." A series of seminars was agreed upon partly to "explore the concepts" and to "outline a conceptual scheme." [36] At the Sigma plant, a training program emphasizing a conceptual scheme developed by Blake initiated the changes, providing the managers at the plant with new ways of conceiving of their experiences and actions.[37] The conceptual framework may not be overtly presented, of course, but may very well be revealed over time through the influencing agent's interpretations and evaluations. In Plant Y, the automobile assembly plant studied by Guest, the new scheme was not formally presented. The new manager met with the plant supervisors in various meetings and told the men "what he believed in." He outlined in writing a long-range program and set up a series of regular meetings to examine their operations. Gradually, the men were brought to "a greater awareness of how the total organization 'fitted together' . . . ." *

Application and Improvisation

Introduction of a new cognitive structure is not sufficient for internalization, however; the individual must actively participate in trying to understand and apply the scheme to his problems. Where internalization does occur, typically the guidelines are general enough that the person being influenced is forced to improvise. Thus the new cognitive structure has to be amplified and integrated into former structures.

At the Nampa Center all four groups had the opportunity

---

* In non-organizational settings, the introduction of a new conception of experience as a part of the internalization process is even more apparent. The religious evangelist presents a world view which explains events in terms of spiritual force and points to the relationships of man's actions to this force. The Communist prison interrogator advances a world view which interprets events as part of a struggle between "progress" and "reaction." From this world view proceeds a prescription of "progressive" and "reactionary" behavior. Different forms of psychotherapy provide a conception of health and sickness which enables the patient to reconceive of his life and supplies him with a consistent way of interpreting his experiences.

to utilize the scheme in their work, but there was a difference in the extent to which each group found it necessary to do so. The Junior Managers and the Senior Scientists placed on the CAPS committees, where there were no superior-subordinate relationships, were given difficult and exacting tasks to perform, and they had to improvise methods for accomplishing these tasks without recourse to positional authority. The Director provided a general scheme, but they had to make the new relationships workable. In doing so, they had to modify his ideas to fit their specific problems and to integrate them with their other patterns of thought and behavior. In a sense, they were forced to make the new scheme "their own" in order to make the committees work at all.

Neither the Senior Managers nor the Junior Scientists were placed in a situation where they were forced to utilize the new scheme. The Senior Managers still worked primarily in a context of previously established relationships. Their contact with others was altered primarily in amount rather than kind; their relationships with the Director and with the Junior Managers were still those of subordinate and superior. The Senior Managers' assignment to engage in long-range planning could have required utilization and improvisation of the scheme, but no concrete objectives or mechanisms were worked out and the assignment was not attempted during this period.

The Junior Scientists as a whole really had no new context which required them to make use of the Director's ideas. Some were left on their own more than before, some were allowed to work in the CAPS committees, but in general they were not in a position in which they had to make the scheme work.

King and Janis in an experiment with college students demonstrated the effectiveness of improvisation for inducing opinion change. Three groups of male students were

Change in Organizations

presented with a written document concerning the induction of graduating college students into the military service, a topic of current importance to them personally. Men in one group were asked only to study the statement. Men in a second group were asked to read it aloud with as much effect as possible so that the statement could be tape-recorded and played to judges. Those in the third group were asked to read the statement and then role-play the part of an advocate of the views stated in the paper. Results of questionnaires filled out several months before and immediately after the experiment showed that only the group who had had to improvise showed a significant opinion change. Moreover, the experimenters' analysis showed that the difference between the groups could not be attributed to closer attention to the written statement or to higher satisfaction with their performance.[38] *

In the organizational studies at Banner, Sigma, and Guest's automobile assembly plant, the supervisors had to improvise to make the suggested ideas operational in their own departments. At Banner the managers and supervisors had to build in their own ideas in order to implement "participation management" in their own part of the plant. At Sigma the men had some idea at the end of the training session of the aims

---

* Schein (*op. cit.*, p. 136) reported that in the Chinese thought-reform prisons, the prisoners were kept under extreme pressure to make a confession of their guilt, but they were not told what the content of the confession was to be. The prisoner had to supply the material for the confession himself. He was only told repeatedly to stop holding back and to make a complete confession. Only then would there be any promise that the pressure would cease. His task was to produce a confession which would demonstrate to the satisfaction of his captors his complete and unqualified acceptance of the Communist scheme of things. To do this he had to improvise with material from his own experience. Usually, false (completely fabricated) confessions were condemned and rejected. For an acceptable selection and interpretation of this material he had to look for cues from his interrogator, from his fellow prisoners who had successfully confessed, and from the controlled mass media. The prisoner had to try repeatedly to demonstrate that he had come to interpret the events in his life in terms of the constructs of his captors.

of the favored management style, but they had to apply the ideas to their own unique situation. At the automobile assembly plant studied by Guest the supervisors were impressed by the way the new manager treated them and by his use of meetings to gather the relevant information and to plan the work. But they had to take his pattern, modify it, and improvise in order to make the new approach work for them.

Verification Through Experience

Testing a new scheme through one's own experience is probably the most important of the three elements of internalization. It is too often overlooked in the rush to examine the irrational aspects of the influence process. The individual adopts the attitude or behavior and gives it meaning independent of the original source, but only as he finds it relevant and valid in working with his own problems. He must test it against the world as he perceives that world.

At Nampa the Junior Managers were told that they would be given greater responsibility. Shortly afterward they were requested to prepare projected budgets, a task formerly performed by the Senior Managers. The Junior Managers were told that they would be the contact men for their projects with Research and Sales, and before long they were assigned to committees with important and urgent tasks with these men. In approximately the same manner, the Senior Scientists were given an open-ended assignment: to make themselves more useful to the line projects. Soon afterward they were assigned as members of CAPS committees where the task was to plan and execute line projects. Specific organizational mechanisms were provided by the Director to help both groups achieve their objectives, and thus they consistently found their experience coinciding with their expectations.

For the other two groups the situation was very different. The Senior Managers' assignment to do long-range technical planning was no more open-ended than the assignments given the two groups just discussed, but no mechanisms were established to implement this difficult assignment. Moreover, the Senior Managers could see that the Director was not in the same power position to support them in their role as long-range planners that he was for the Junior Managers and Senior Scientists in their new roles. The Senior Managers were being asked to exert influence in an organizational province at the Director's level or above.

Though the situation for the Junior Scientists was different, the net result was the same. The Director did have the power to support his assertion that the changes would give the Junior Scientists more responsibility and autonomy, but he provided no specific organizational mechanisms to help bring this about.

At Banner experimenters first introduced participative management in an industrial engineering project; efficiency rose and morale remained high. So later they set up an experimental department and again the early results were close enough to those anticipated that the superintendents in the plant chose to extend the new management methods to other departments. At Plant Y the supervisors tried new methods of running their departments and produced better results. Following the new manager's lead in holding regular meetings, they found it possible to coordinate their efforts better. They took chances, made mistakes, and were not fired. In recommending technical changes they found each change gave them "that much more chance to think ahead so we won't get in the hole next time." At Sigma the management at the plant drew heavily on the approaches developed in the Grid Laboratory sessions in deciding how to handle a manpower reduction, and the results were so encouraging

that they sought to use the approach on more of their operating problems.*

In one sense, this part of the internalization process may
be termed reality-testing, but this is not to say that uniform
views of reality prevail. Indeed, an individual's perception
of reality may be distorted, but for an individual to integrate the new construct into his system of beliefs he must
validate it through his perception of reality.

SUMMARY

Examining each of these preconditions and dimensions
separately makes it easy to lose sight of the whole. This is
unfortunate for it is the total process that is important. The
features described do not exist separately in the actual situation. A brief summary of these features of the process of
change may serve to re-emphasize that they are parts of a
single phenomenon.

Two prior conditions are necessary to facilitate the initiation of change: (1) the presence of tension, and (2) a powerful influencing agent. If an individual is experiencing tension, if he is dissatisfied with the status quo, or if he is unsuccessful in achieving his aims, he is much more likely to be
influenced successfully by a respected, prestigeful individual,

---

* In each of the above instances, the new scheme found confirmation in
the individual's experience, but there is also the other side of the coin. One
of the striking outcomes of the Chinese thought-reform program among
western prisoners is that, among most returned prisoners, it did *not* produce
long-range ideological changes independent of the external support provided
in the prison setting. Only a very few former prisoners maintained an
espousal of the ideological position "taught" in the prison after they had had
time to re-evaluate the prison experience and had new sources of information which they could check. (Schein and Bennis, *op. cit.*, pp. 157–166.) What
would have happened to these prisoners had they returned to a Communist
society is impossible to say, but where the viewpoint of his captors failed
to find validation in the prisoner's experience after the prison experience, it
was not internalized. Of course, in those areas where the Chinese captors'
schema *did* continue to be congruent with their experience, the change in
the ex-prisoners' attitudes and behavior continued to be affected.

whom he sees as a source of help. Even given these conditions, however, an individual is unlikely to maintain the changed attitude or behavior, unless (1) the goals and objectives toward which he is working become increasingly specific and concrete; (2) the relationships which reinforce his former attitudes and behavior are altered or severed, and he establishes new relationships supportive of the change; (3) his self-esteem is heightened in the process of change; and (4) he internalizes the content of the motive for change as he develops new perceptions of his situation, improvises to make the schema fit his situation, and confirms the validity and utility of the new schema through his own experience.

The power of the new Director to induce change at the Nampa Center lay partly in the authority of his formal position, the support of his superiors, and his reputation for achievement at the Center. It lay partly in the fact that there was tension at the Center and an expectation that the new Director would provide leadership in relieving the sources of this tension. But the intended changes in behavior and attitudes were successfully established only where mechanisms were introduced which facilitated movements along each of these dimensions. The CAPS program established a vehicle which provided the Junior Managers and Senior Scientists with increasingly specific objectives, a basis for establishing new relationships, and an opportunity for new accomplishments, and a situation sufficiently open-ended to allow them to test out new roles. No similar mechanisms were available to the Senior Managers and Junior Scientists to enable movement in these directions.

CHAPTER VI

Conclusion

THIS STUDY of change in formal organization structure examined how a top manager altered the distribution of authority and simultaneously reorganized the centers of power and influence in a research and development activity. The objective of the change was to increase productivity through the heightened motivation of individuals closely connected with the project work of the Center. Shifting authority downward in the organization and altering the bases of power and influence resulted in increased importance of work groups and diminished importance of departments as the units of planning and decision making. It resulted also in added power and visibility of selected middle managers and professional scientists at the expense of the two senior levels of management just below the position of the chief executive of the Center.

This study therefore deals directly with a problem basic in all formal organization planning: the social-psychological consequences of decisions to reallocate authority and to alter the means by which individuals seek to influence one another. This problem, as it appears in a research and development center, sharply portrays the tensions inherent in all organizations as alternate types of authority compete for power and influence.

STRUCTURAL CHANGE AND ALTERNATE TYPES OF AUTHORITY

Two major types of authority upon which power relations develop are hierarchical and professional. Hierarchical authority vests power, or the potential for influencing others, in

PUBLISHER'S NOTE: This chapter was written by Professor Zaleznik. See Foreword.

individuals who occupy specific positions in organizations. Hierarchical or positional authority is far from an antiquated base for influencing men. But for influence to occur in a hierarchy, members must accord recognition and prior willingness to accept influence from above. This point, called variously legitimacy and the consent of the governed, is itself a rational process. Men consent to be governed because they recognize the necessity for hierarchical leadership and, even more significantly, judge its potential uses to themselves and their groups insofar as leadership produces effective actions in regulating relations with the environment. The exercise of hierarchical authority has to result in more effective organizations — the production of a surplus of rewards over costs — to enchance the value of membership in an organization.

The significance and vitality of hierarchical authority lie not so much in traditions and the willingness of men to go along with authority figures, but more in the demonstrated capacity of people at the top to secure decisions and to move the organization in a productive direction. Every member of an organization is therefore capable of evaluating how effectively authority figures use power. The issue of legitimacy of hierarchical authority certainly in the long run is less ideological and more pragmatic than is suggested by those who distrust hierarchical authority. If "power corrupts and absolute power corrupts absolutely," it also lends direction to men's efforts and provides the rewards which sustain their willingness to accept influence.

The issue of effectiveness of hierarchical authority bears strongly in this study. The head of the development center assumed the top position in an organization which had a questionable reputation in the eyes both of its members and of corporate authority figures who approved its budget and otherwise lent continuity to its existence. A moribund research and development activity in a technologically sophisticated industry and society lives a precarious existence. It was not within the power of members to effect a change in the organization. For organization change to have occurred required some decision from corporate headquarters to establish a position and an incumbent who represented clearly the intention to alter the organization's capabilities and performance.

Generally speaking, there are two clear-cut techniques for accelerating change in an organization: (1) bringing in new people (and letting old ones go), and (2) changing the formal organization structure. The Director of the Center availed himself of both techniques, although in this research we concentrated attention on the change in formal organization structure.

But we must inquire into the rationale for proposing and justifying a new design of formal organization, which brings us to the second base of authority, professional expertise. Here, the representations, communications, and perceptions of influence depend upon the visibility and potential uses of expert knowledge. These influence transactions are founded upon a bedrock of rationality in that professional expertise should result in the solution of problems and successful adaptation to the environment. The acceptance of professional expertise may exist initially on faith (i.e., "the willing suspension of disbelief"), or on acceptance of credentials. But here again in the long run the willingness to follow an expert's lead is founded upon demonstrated performance.

It is just on this point, however, that we face a serious contradiction in the management of organizations. Rational evaluations maintain authority and power in organizations, yet it is exceedingly difficult to demonstrate rationally the superiority of a particular organization design as the preferred structure of authority relations. An individual can argue, as did the Director of the Center in this study, that a flat organization is more conducive to effective technical work groups than the pyramid, or that it will bring technical specializations to bear more fruitfully in achieving project goals. The arguments may seem plausible and reasonable, but there still remains ground for doubt. There is little internal evidence which can be marshaled to prove the validity of arguments justifying a particular organization structure. In one sense, the arguments are rationalizations for a predetermined course of action, although they may be presented in objective terms to convince others to accept the intended change.

What becomes strikingly clear in the final analysis is that the occupant of the top position uses the power he derives from hierarchical authority to alter the organization structure and thereby to change the distribution of authority, both quantitative and qualitative, throughout the organization. In the case under investigation the change distributed authority downward ("flattened" the organization) to secure a shift in the power structure in favor of the technical specialists over higher levels of line management. In this organization change, as in most others, hierarchical authority initiated the shift in the structure of authority relationships and, as we shall demonstrate presently, it was toward hierarchical authority that the ultimate balance of power returned.

It is quite clear that the underlying saliency to the change in this study stemmed from two facts: (1) that it was introduced by a new top man who had secured the support of corporate headquarters, and (2) that it was sufficiently different from the existing pattern to create new anticipations. This second fact requires some scrutiny and brings into focus some of the conflicts generated in using hierarchical authority to change the formal distribution of authority through a new organization structure.

We indicated earlier that hierarchical authority must prove its effectiveness for it to sustain itself and be available for

fresh attempts at influencing behavior. The "willing suspension of disbelief" is at best a temporary phenomenon
binding those led to their leaders. Sooner or later the rational
weighing of rewards and costs of a given power structure
strengthens the bonds of authority where returns are favorable or weakens them where costs exceed rewards. Individuals then begin to search for alternatives and to withdraw
their emotional investments from the organization and its
symbols of authority.

The weighing of rewards and costs is a rational process and
becomes salient in those aspects of work life involving the
individual's commitments. We can distinguish in the psychology of organizations two kinds of emotional involve-
ments: one type centers on an attitude of compliance and
the second on active commitment. The attitude of compliance exists in those spheres of decision where a wide range of
alternative solutions are equally acceptable to individuals
and group members. Hours of work, physical conditions,
and various procedures governing the routine of daily work
life lend themselves to a number of satisfactory solutions.
So long as minimum limits of expectancy are met, there is
little concern about the particular techniques employed.
Herzberg in his studies of job satisfaction refers to these areas
of work life as the hygienic factors — the absence of acceptable
solutions leads to job dissatisfaction while their presence
does not provide positive job satisfaction.[1] The organization
theorist Chester Barnard also referred to the psychological
process of compliance through his concept of "the zone of indifference."[2] One implication of this concept in Barnard's
work suggests shifting areas of decision making so that they
fall into the individual's zone of indifference. If this practice were possible, it would result in a maximum number of
options for managers with the highest assurance that whatever option the manager selects, it would be acceptable in the
organization.

It would be fair to say that the problem of managing authority relations at the professional and managerial levels stems directly from the fact that the areas of compliance are few in number and precisely absent in those activities which occupy most of the manager's time and emotional energy. Instead, he is dealing directly with the second class of problems, involving the significant commitments of men to their work and career.

The striking fact about professional careers (and we would include managerial as well as technical specialties in this category) is the cogency of the encounter between inner and outer aspects of performance. The psychological processes of development in the adult interact with the objective components of work, including not only the exercise of technical competence but also the qualities of the organization and of the persons with whom one works. This encounter, referred to as the individual's role-task work, has been described in the following way by Hodgson, Levinson, and Zaleznik:

> The term "role-task" denotes the linkage between a man's assessment of his personality, his here-and-now conception of himself, and his assessment of the requirements of his position in the organization . . . a melding of organizational imperatives and personal strivings.

> Briefly, *role-task work* is the sustained and directed effort of mind in which a person seeks to synthesize the organizational requirements of his position with his own individual needs, interests, and aspirations. The result of successful role-task work is a set of personal policies, as it were, by which the person strives to advance, or *impede* the purposes of the organization, depending on his needs. Role-task work is seen as an active, ongoing process engaged in by the individual. It is a basic requisite of productive membership within an organization. This idea about man-in-organization points to the person-position encounter as highly problematic; it cannot be taken for granted in a theoretical sense, although

it may often be conveniently ignored in purposive situations that are functioning smoothly.[3]

Clearly a momentous developmental problem occurs for the individual when he is faced with the task of designing or reacting to a new organizational structure. The process of role-task work, involving the individual's major commitments to career, is heightened and in essence describes the inner aspects of organizational change. The individual cannot allow decisions to go by default, and even if he appears to define organizational change in the realm of decisions to which he complies, such as the case of the Junior Scientists in this study, he is still scrutinizing actions and reactions of authority figures for the potential answers to his future role-task concerns.

From the standpoint of the chief executive of an organization, the issues of individual role-task work (apart from his own) are manifestly of secondary importance in designing and implementing a formal organization structure. He seemingly adopts a program in the interests of furthering the goals of the organization, but central to his program is the effort to resolve certain problems of power and authority, not the least of which include his own, and to establish a balance of favorable response to assure at least the initiation of his program.

The effects of "flattening" the organization structure are to eliminate certain managerial positions and to alter others drastically. The efforts initially consist of a new quantitative distribution of authority along with a shift in the primacy of one type of authority over another. In this case, the quantitative shift curtailed the authority of the Senior Managers and their immediate subordinates, whose jobs were eliminated. While the Senior Managers' positions still existed, they were out of the mainstream of the influence process by virtue of their inaccessibility to job planning and work evaluation in the form of CAPS group meetings, budget discussions, and project review with top management. Their time allocations were supposed to shift from interaction with subordinates to the vague activity called "long-range planning." Qualitatively, the balance between positional and professional authority was supposed to shift in favor of professional authority through more direct presence of Senior Scientists in project planning and development. The Senior Scientists had no positional authority but instead were to function as staff specialists contributing expertise to development projects.

The case of the Junior Managers presented an interesting problem in fusing positional and professional authority. As engineers with significant records of technical accomplishment, they were to direct project work. The bases of their power and influence left an option open to each Junior Manager. He could structure his work relationships on the basis of his technical expertise or, as an administrator who acts as the link between technical experts and top management, and in general facilitates the work of others through securing resources for the group. Where the technical expert leads groups through directive guidance and control of work, the administrator delegates technical direction in favor of mediating and balancing the inner workings of the group with external authority.

As we have seen in the data presentations of Chapter IV, those most clearly affected by the change through enhancement of their authority base expressed considerable support for the new organization structure (Senior Scientists and Junior Managers). Negative sentiments appeared where a clear deprivation existed in the weakening of the authority base of the Senior Managers. The results were mixed in the case of Junior Scientists, depending mainly upon whether Junior Managers continued the distribution of authority downward, or whether as technical experts they maintained directive control of projects. In those cases where Junior Managers emphasized technical expertise of subordinates in influencing work decisions, attitudes of Junior Scientists appeared favorable to the change.

In discussing who benefits and who is deprived in the shifting authority structure, we arrive at the crucial factor which determines whether a new organization structure gains initial acceptance despite the absence of objective means for relating intentions with outcomes.

A new formal organization structure represents implicitly, if not explicitly, a coalition of interests in which the redistribution of authority determines the lines of support for the new plan. It is clear from this study that flattening the organization structure benefited lower status managers and professionals but not at the expense of the chief executive. He enhanced his total power at the expense of the middle level managers whose jobs were eliminated or altered.[4] His enhanced power came from accumulating and directly relating resources to those who need and consume the budgetary allocations. His power was also enhanced through being more intimately involved in appraising technical performances and having a wider knowledge of work activity, ultimately adding to his capacity to shape the opinions of his superiors.

In effect, to decentralize or "flatten" the organization involved a *de facto* coalition among the Director of the Center, the staff specialists (Senior Scientists), and heads of autonomous work groups (Junior Managers). The chief executive used hierarchical authority to alter the authority structure in favor of professional authority, but in the course of doing so enhanced his own positional authority by making himself strategic in accumulating and distributing resources throughout the organization, thereby regulating the flow of work.

We can conclude therefore that in assessing responses to change in organization structure, the critical issues have to do with gains and losses in power and the consequences for the individual in his role-task work. If an individual's authority base is enhanced, he responds favorably and in effect joins a coalition in support of a new formal organization structure. The intervening variable between organizational change and the response of the individual is the nature of the role-task work which must take place during the course of and immediately following the introduction of the new plan. The nature and outcome of the role-task work is by no means obvious even though the correlation between enhanced authority and attitude is positive.

The change calls upon individuals to formulate a personal plan as a response to change not of their own initiation. It is important to recognize that no matter how much people discuss a change program in advance, participate in its formulation, and even come to feel that they had something to do with introducing the change, these terms may only disguise the fact that initiation comes from the top figure and the responses have to do with anticipations of increases or decreases in one's base of power.

THEORIES OF ORGANIZATION

Classical scientific management and administrative theory [5] take as their central concern the problem of rationalizing work and its organization structure. These theories of work and organization operate on the principle of establishing in advance of performance the methods of work and areas of responsibility for each position in the structure. The problem of establishing and relating separate functions into a coherent whole defines the term rationalization in organization planning.

The manifest intention of rationalization is to direct energy in quantity, time, and place according to an overall plan of organization function at all status levels. The latent effect, of course, is the centralization of management control in a

hierarchy of line and staff positions. Authority and power
flow downward in executing plans and in rewarding performance.

In classical theory the critical behavior expected from
those who execute predetermined actions in contrast to those
who make plans is compliance to directives. Compliance in
organizations and therefore the effectiveness of the rationalized organization structures hypothetically occur under any
one of the following conditions:

1. When the rewards for fulfilling expectations are greater
    than costs in expending effort or in foregoing alternatives.[6]
2. When the expected behavior falls within the individual's
    zone of indifference,[7] which means that he has no prefer-
    ence for one set of actions over another in expending
    energy.
3. When a felt identity of interests exists between those who
    plan and those who execute activities.

Three major developments historically challenged the
adequacy of the classical theory. The first development, the
emergence of collective bargaining among employees, acted
as a countervailing force to offset the power of managers who
created and implemented rationalized organization structures. The assumption of identity of interests to assure compliance could no longer be maintained, leading to the search
for new theories and ideologies of organization.

The second development took the form of the human relations movement following the Hawthorne and Group Dynamics experiments.[8] This school of thought introduced
new variables concerning the motivation to work, particularly in its emphasis on informal organization, group cohesion, and person-oriented management.

Finally, the third development in back of the search for
new theories of organization was the entry into industry of
the professional employee, and the shift in interest from the

blue collar to the professional employee, and to the manager himself. As we indicated earlier, the difference between the professional and nonprofessional employee is in attitudes toward work and career. The professional views his work as an issue of commitment to a career rather than compliance to particular organizational imperatives. In this sense the professional operates from a power base which depends upon the unique value of his training and expertise rather than the force of collective bargaining. Decisions to perform in certain ways bear a strong relation to the individual's concept of his career and the relevance of day-to-day activity to long-range personal goals.

Human relations research presents a view of organizations different from the classical schools of administrative theory and scientific management. Instead of emphasizing formal organization structures in the rationalization of work, it emphasizes the existence of the informal organization. Workers and managers evolve a set of activities and relationships which utilize the formal structure but which also transcend the constraints of required activities and interactions. Informal ranking patterns grow out of the formal status structure established in the design of organizations. The spontaneously chosen leader of work groups exerts influence parallel and even in opposition to the formally designated supervisor. In addition to directed work activity, employees engage in certain nonwork or purely social events which are as patterned and persistent as the work requirements of organizations.[9]

The central variable in human relations studies is the motivation of the employee in contradiction to the assumption of economic man as the constant motivating force leading to compliance with directives. Motives derive from man's social nature and his desire for communication and a sense of personal well-being. Insofar as rationalized organization structures ignore human and social needs, the informal organization provides the missing gratifications and as a consequence creates a parallel authority structure.

The prescriptive notions of the human relations school emphasize the role of the leader. Through permissive and person-centered attitudes the leader fosters group cohesion and ultimately the satisfaction of social as well as economic needs.

Despite the many differences between the rationalistic and human relations theories and approaches, several striking similarities stand out. It is not at all clear, for example, that the human relations theories aim at anything different from compliance with directives which is characteristic of the classical theories. The ideas of participative management and permissiveness would seem to shift some of the authority and control downward in the hierarchy, but in the final analysis these techniques appear more as psychological rituals and less as substantive shifts in the balance of power. If the employee feels a sense of participation through group discussion methods, he will comply with plans which are generated at the top of the hierarchy and flow downward.[10] The real shift in organization is the method of introducing change rather than reliance on an attitude toward authority different from compliance.

More recent approaches in the human relations school would seem to suggest a substantive shift in the distribution of authority. The use of more sophisticated group techniques, like work groups modeled after the T-Group[11] or McGregor's Theory Y,[12] are expressions of egalitarian ideals, particularly the sharing of authority and power. But autonomy and dependency are complex psychological phenomena. Whenever a theory of management increases the disparity between formal status, or the authority of position, and the ideals of power and influence, increased dependency and reduced autonomy may well follow. The condition of ambiguity resulting from this tension may in effect reduce the

capacity of individuals to influence their environment and as
a corollary may increase the power of authority figures.

RATIONALITY IN ORGANIZATIONAL BEHAVIOR

Placing the significance of classical and human relations
theories and their impact on power relations in organizations
in historical perspective raises for consideration in a new
light the nature of rationality in organizational behavior.
Organizations are fundamentally instruments of human action. They exist for the achievement of explicit purposes and
ideally depend upon a consistent relationship between means
and ends. Organization structure and the directives supporting it are the means through which goals are to be achieved.

The fact that research studies show the existence of extra-
organizational phenomena like cliques, informal leaders,
and unwritten codes of behavior does not negate the intended
rationality of formal organizations. Nor is it correct to view
the emerging social behavior in organizations as "nonrational" elements which necessarily destroy the means-ends
relationship of formal organization.

The basis for describing informal organization as nonrational is its spontaneous character and existence outside the
directives of formal planning. The explanation of informal
organization as the mechanism for satisfying social needs
through interpersonal relations also suggests a nonrational
quality. Here the criterion for using rational or nonrational
is simply whether behavior fits in the means-ends structure
of work organization. But if we re-examine rationality in the
light of issues of authority and power, as evidenced in this
study, there are grounds for suggesting that formal organization has both rational and nonrational components along
with informal organization.

We are indebted for clarification of the issues of rationality
in organizations to a recent work of the French sociologist

Michel Crozier and his book, *The Bureaucratic Phenomenon*.[13] Crozier suggests, and demonstrates empirically, that informal organization also grows out of the realities of authority and the distribution of power in work structures. The formation of coalitions, the control of output, and the exchanges within and between groups can be interpreted as efforts at securing effective power and control.[14] Groups build upon complementary interests and establish regulations in decision making to protect group interests and existing internal ranking structures. Resistance to changes occurs mainly when the effect of change is to alter the balance of power in the organization without offsetting compensations.

Formal organization planning and the decision to change the structure of authority proceed at two distinct levels. The first level deals directly with the means-ends problem and is distinctly rational. This level is concrete and includes the decision to accumulate manpower, equipment, and other resources necessary to produce specific kinds of goods and services. Its current symbol is the budget, which in detail specifies the relationship of inputs to outputs. The second level problem in organizational planning is the grouping of functions, establishing authority relations in the form of lines of accountability, and establishing mechanisms for coordination. This problem concerns directly the overall design of the formal organization. Close examination of this problem, particularly in the distribution of authority, suggests, as we have indicated earlier, a range of possibilities, all of which can be rationalized, but none of which is rational in the same sense as the first order problem where it is possible to demonstrate an optimal relationship of means and ends at the concrete level of technologies, resources, operations, and products. It is difficult if not impossible in any given situation to demonstrate in rational terms how one particular organization structure yields a higher payoff than another. What can be demonstrated in the rationalizations of an organization structure is: (1) that a proposed plan is different from others in the distribution of authority; (2) that it will benefit some individuals and groups in the balance of power; (3) that plans similar to the one proposed are used elsewhere and seem to work satisfactorily. Beyond these demonstrable features a formal structure in the final analysis represents one design of organization, among a number of options, in which the authority figure invests his confidence as his solution to the second level problem. Viewed in this way, formal organization is also nonrational and governed by complex social-psychological forces, including the motivations of the top executive and his style of leadership.

EVALUATING EMPIRICAL EVIDENCE

The nonrational character of formal organization structure is especially significant in the management of research and development organizations as well as in other enterprises which depend upon creative efforts of men. There is no way to assert a logic to establish in advance the relation between a plan and desired goals. Above all, there is no logic to deal with the hard fact that in changing the formal organization structure, shifts occur in authority and power leading to relative gains and losses for individuals and groups.

The absence of conventional rationality in the problem of formal organization planning makes it difficult to evaluate the effects of change on stated goals. One problem for research is essentially to uncover the latent social-psychological forces which determine, and result from, change. Significant forces cluster around the motives of leaders in altering authority relations and the effects of change on the inner role-task concerns and outer behavior of the members of the organization in response to gains and losses in authority.

Studies of the social psychology of authority and power

relations and alterations in formal organization structure are presently all too scarce in the literature. It is therefore premature to present prescriptions or recommendations on the uses of different types of organization structures. In concluding this research report, therefore, it seems appropriate to present and discuss a series of propositions which can stand as inferences and interpretations of the empirical results of this study. These propositions also can serve as material for further empirical work and theoretical discussion.

Propositions

1. Alteration in the formal organization structure is a necessary but not sufficient condition to shift the balance of authority and power in the direction of intentions.
2. Shifts in authority and power tend to occur when mechanisms which alter patterns of interaction, decision making, and evaluation accompany change in organization structure.

These two propositions state the conditions under which change in formal organization structure tends to shift authority, power, and influence. A change in the structure without the mechanisms reflected in new modes of interacting and evaluating work leaves the individual to whom authority is supposed to be transferred without the tools for expressing and representing to others his intentions to use the authority. The intervening variable between structural change and a new actual balance of power is the individual role-task work which results in the conversion of structural authority to power and influence. The role-task work necessary to support a new authority structure may fail for a variety of reasons related to individual motivation, but even assuming that the motivation is present, the mechanisms to make authority operational in work transactions are a necessary condition for transferring the intentions of a structure into the behavior of individuals.

3. Changes in organization structure create new identity of interests among individuals in different statuses, groups, and occupations corresponding to their relative gains and losses in authority and power.

4. Individuals whose authority increases as a result of changes in organization structure tend to develop positive attitudes toward the change and support its implementation. Conversely, a reduction in relative authority leads to dissatisfaction.

5. Hierarchical authority is the central legitimate force for introducing changes. Responses to change and the hierarchical authority which initiates change depend upon the power available in the coalitions of interest which form as a consequence of gains and losses in authority.

The initial acceptance of a new organization structure requires a *de facto* coalition among individuals who stand to gain in authority and power as a result of a new organization structure. If for any reason the coalition fails to form, such as a communication blockage or the opposing forces of conflicting interests, then a new structure is not likely to gain even the initial acceptance necessary to implement a plan. We have argued that conventional rationality of organizational structure at the levels above work groups is either nonexistent or difficult to establish and communicate. Within a range of reasonable alternatives, the favored organization structure can be defined as the one which succeeds in building a viable coalition of interests at several status levels. The nucleus of this coalition is the chief executive of an organization who represents and utilizes hierarchical authority. The idea for a new organization or the motivation for a new plan does not have to start with the chief executive, but any successful coalition short of overturning the existing authority structure requires the power of the man representative of hierarchical authority.

6. Changes in organization structure increase expectations and heighten tensions for individuals who anticipate enhanced authority and power.
7. Dissatisfactions increase as a result of formal organization change in proportion to the discrepancy between expectations and outcomes in the realization of authority and power.

It is easy to explain the dissatisfactions of individuals who lose authority and power following change in the formal organization structure. The case of individuals who neither gain nor lose, yet experience as much dissatisfaction as those who suffer a real deprivation, is more subtle. This phenomenon of dissatisfaction following heightened expectation with limited realization of rewards is now well established in understanding the condition of deprived and supposedly mobile populations. The same general effect seems to occur in formal organizations.

The promises of change, even if indirect, seem to stimulate men's desires. In the face of limited new rewards or a longer time span than anticipated in their realization, a sense of frustration often takes hold. In many cases, this delayed reaction to change is the negative fallout of efforts to alter work relationships for some desired ends and little can be done to prevent its appearance. This problem may be overcome in due course as individual performance gains recognition; it is not easily dissolved in those situations where the performance is undistinguished. The net effect of dissatisfactions resulting from unfulfilled expectations may be resistance to change on the part of those individuals who become cynical as well as those individuals who have managed to gain power but fear its loss in the face of new changes in the authority structure.

8. Resistance to change proportional to the reduction in authority and power is a rational response to anticipated consequences of change.

9. Rational resistance to change by itself is neutral with respect to the content of organizational change — it neither supports nor detracts from the wisdom of undertaking a paiticular change effort.

Earlier we distinguished between rationality at the level of the organization and the group. The two are different and worthy of careful analysis. It is possible to establish rationality of action at the organizational level when dealing with the comparison of inputs and outputs; it is highly difficult when dealing with actions involving the more abstract issues of management, such as the desired structure of authority.

Establishing rationality at the level of the individual is both more practical and more immediate as compared with organizational rationality: as individuals experience relative losses in authority and power, the rational response of resistance is in keeping with the experience of deprivation. At a minimum, a conflict of interest exists between those who initiate change and those who experience the conditions of altered work structures.

The change may be the best available solution to the organization's problems in the eyes of its chief executive and still confront selected members with personal losses. The usual practice in the face of conflicts of interest is negotiation and bargaining with the final step of separation between the conflicting parties always a distinct possibility. Bargaining is a rational procedure in the face of conflict; the denial of conflict is irrational as is the assertion of priority of the organization's interests over that of the individual. The organization's interests may prevail, but only as an outcome of its superior bargaining position. In the case of individuals whose services are valued highly, their potential losses in a change program will usually merit considerable attention if not lead outright to modification in the planned changes.

A more difficult problem occurs when proposals for change are founded upon or encounter irrational evaluations. In the case of the organization, irrationality exists when a proposal for change is justified as an absolute or on grounds beyond existing capacities to establish relationships between means and ends. At the level of the individual, irrationality occurs when responses involve a sense of deprivation when no shift in the balance of power occurs in reality. Irrationality at the levels of the organization and the individual are distinctly unamenable to bargaining and represent in effect the pathological concomitants of change.

In Conclusion

The thrust of this research on the actions of management in changing the formal organization structure shifts attention away from simple evaluations of outcomes and toward understanding the nature of power relations in management. In bringing together theories of authority, power, and influence into a dynamic conception, organization structure becomes more a problem of man acting in social situations and less the idealized forms of relationships which result from some impersonal way of relating means and ends. Between the initiation of an organization structure and the outcomes stand the processes through which individuals assess themselves in relation to an external structure and undertake actively to shape their position and roles to conform to personal career management. Even, or especially, in the design of formal organization structures, the personal meanings of the structure to top management become central variables for investigation.

While there are distinct and obvious limits to the generalizations which this study has yielded, it does suggest a new range of investigations into formal organization as an aspect of executive action, a topic largely neglected in empirical studies of business.

CHAPTER VII

Another Point of View

WHEN several individuals collaborate on a research study, they have the advantage of pooled efforts and the stimulation of different viewpoints. During the phases of research design, data collection, and data analysis, these separate viewpoints can generate fruitful analyses and competing hypotheses. These in turn can lead to further inquiry and study.

However, researchers in any field are only human. Each person brings his own values, experience, and point of view to the interpretation of data. Differences of opinion inevitably arise around what the data actually "mean." Some of this disagreement is data based. Some of it resides in the psychological needs for primacy and self-justification inherent in the researchers. The problem then is what to do.

In this case, differences occurred over several interpretations and conclusions. They were apparently irreconcilable. Consequently, Professor Zaleznik, as the senior member of the research team, drafted Chapter VI as one concluding chapter and wishes to keep that chapter intact without change. Much of Chapter VI "makes sense" to us. Other parts of Chapter VI make assumptions that puzzle us. We wish to question these and to put up alternative possibilities in this chapter.

For example, Chapter VI assumes that organizational design involves a range of possibilities "all of which can be rationalized, but none of which is rational" in ways that are demonstrably superior. According to this reasoning, one organizational design is as good as another, actually governed

PUBLISHER'S NOTE: This chapter was written by Professors Barnes and Dalton. See Foreword.

by the "latent social-psychological forces which determine and result from change." In addition, a manager's manifest reasons for making an organizational change in structure are rationalizations while "central to his program is the effort to resolve certain problems of power and authority, not the least of which include his own." Later on Chapter VI notes that "flattening the organization structure benefited lower status managers and professionals, but not at the expense of the chief executive . . ." who "enhanced his own positional authority by making himself strategic in . . . regulating the flow of work."

These conclusions pose problems for us and, we imagine, for some readers. To begin with, it seems reasonable to assume that organizational design is a combination of rational objectives and rationalization. To accept the premise in Chapter VI that all such plans can be rationalized but none is rational is to deny both managerial experience and a growing wealth of behavioral science research. One can certainly argue that such research is "so thin as to make unwarranted the blanket advocacy of programs and ideologies" as Professor Zaleznik does in Chapter I, but this provides scant argument for rejecting research findings as part of a rational organizational design process. The accumulated research suggests that certain organizational structures and procedures *do* tend to accompany certain task environments and *are* optimal for certain specified outcomes. Part of the research will be reviewed briefly in this chapter.

A second problem comes up around Dr. West's latent motives for proposing and implementing the Nampa design. There is no question of the importance of latent motives in determining Dr. West's or anyone else's behavior. However, Chapter VI dismisses the possibility of making a rational argument for a given change in the organizational structure and suggests that any such arguments are necessarily manifest rationalizations covering a latent bid for power. There is no real evidence we can find to support such a position. Instead, we suggest that *both* manifest and latent goals were important to Dr. West, and that his goals included a gain in Nampa's total power and not merely personal power seeking. Data in Chapter II suggest that Dr. West considered the Nampa Center an open rather than a closed system; one in which the amount of power available was a variable sum rather than a fixed sum. In this sense, Dr. West's plan may have been optimistic, for Nampa seems to have had both open and closed system characteristics. But the evidence suggests that he was interested in expanding total power, not just in enhancing his own power at the expense of others. It was more than a rationalization designed to meet his own latent needs for power. There was an organizational reality as well as a psychological reality. The organizational reality would suggest that there was rationality behind Dr. West's manifest goals to:

1. Reduce project stretchouts and delays.
2. Improve the utilization of technical abilities.
3. Move project responsibility downward.
4. Improve long-range technical planning.
5. Improve morale, particularly among staff specialists.

Not only was there an organizational reality underlying these goals, but given Dr. West's assumptions, there was no necessary conflict between his manifest intentions to improve the operations of the Center and any latent intent to improve his own power. He assumed that his own power would increase if others also gained greater influence, autonomy, and involvement. He further assumed that it was possible for those to increase for other parties simultaneously. Consequently, his manifest plan for increasing the organization's effectiveness was consistent with and built upon his efforts to build his own power *and* the power of others. The question remains, however, as to whether an assumption of power expansion is reasonable. The issue was lightly touched upon in Chapter III.

> One of the controversial issues in organization theory centers on the question of whether it is possible to create changes where everyone gains power while the effectiveness of the organization also increases. If the notion smacks of utopianism, it is nevertheless a strong influence on current experimentation in organizations. . . . This speculation comes under question on the grounds that the crucial issue affecting power is the relative distribution of authority.

Within the context of this chapter, the above statement needs qualification. Just as we find it necessary to examine both latent *and* manifest concerns; with nonrational *and* rational factors influencing design of organizations, so do we opt for consideration of both total power *and* relative power. Chapter VI pursues the thesis that relative power alone should be considered. We think it more fruitful to assume the importance of both. Other researchers increasingly share this assumption. For example, Tannenbaum (1968) states that:

> Most analyses of control have been concerned with the *relative* control exercised by groups within organizations rather than the total amount. The literature therefore provides relatively little guidance concerning the conditions under which the amount of control in a system may expand.[1]

The fact that managers (e.g., Dr. West) make an assumption about power expansion is seen as a crucial issue by Tannenbaum. A manager who assumes that total power is a variable will act quite differently from one concerned only with his own relative power.

> Assumptions about control in organizations will have practical consequences since organizational leaders who hold these assumptions are likely to act on the basis of them . . . . the choice of assumptions may lead to self-fulfilling prophe-

sies. For example, the assumption by organization members
of a fixed amount of control may lead to attempts by some
members to restrict the power of others, thus in fact limit-
ing the amount of control within the system. Furthermore,
it seems reasonable to think that the "fixed pie" assumption
and the self-fulfilling consequences contribute to an assumption of basic and prevailing conflict within the organization
and to attempts by leaders to exercise unilateral control —
just as the assumption of prevailing conflict is likely to lead
to attempts by some parties to limit the power of others.[2]

Another pair of writers, Walton and McKersie (1965),
adopt a position akin to our own and unlike Chapter VI's
"fixed pie" assumption. They assume the possibility of *both*
fixed pie and variable pie conditions. In describing labor
negotiations, they picture: (a) distributive bargaining in
which zero-sum conditions exist; gains for one party involve
corresponding losses for the other; (b) integrative bargaining
which pertains under conditions permitting a significantly
varying total, even though both parties may not share equal
gains or losses; the important point is that both parties share
high gains with little sacrifice or vice versa. Finally, (c) mixed
bargaining occurs with potential for both distributive and
integrative bargaining. Whether the bargaining develops
along distributive, integrative, or mixed motive lines depends partly upon the assumptions and actions of the parties
involved.

Having moved through the foregoing conceptual tangle,
we would suggest the following premises for the reader's
consideration:

1. Most organizational situations tend toward mixed
agenda characteristics. This means that they are a complex
combination of zero-sum and non-zero-sum worlds depending
partly upon the latent assumptions held by organizational
members and their colleague-adversaries. The relationships
between these parties seem crucial.

2. Therefore, in examining power in an organization the relationship between members within the organization and with others in the environment deserves more attention than the attributes held by any single member or group. A power relationship involves power on the one hand and dependency on the other. To understand a power relationship, one must also understand the accompanying dependency relationship.

3. Dr. West sought to increase total power in Nampa by expanding dependency within the organization and with others in the environment. In the cases of the Junior Managers, the Senior Scientists, and Dr. West, the power-dependency exchange increased. In the cases of the Senior Managers and most Junior Scientists, it did not.

The first premise we make on "mixed systems" is the one discussed earlier in this chapter. It has guided us in our concerns for *both* manifest *and* latent, rational *and* nonrational, closed system *and* open system, zero-sum *and* non-zero-sum, total power *and* relative power, etc. It has its philosophical basis in the Hegelian dialectic, and it assumes that for every thesis there will be an antithesis and an emerging synthesis. A "mixed system" is the inevitable synthesis in organizations. But whereas Chapter VI stressed latent motives, nonrational behavior, closed system assumptions, and zero-sum relative power, we have tried to encompass the other side, the antithesis, in order to stress the importance of *both* aspects in each case.

The second premise draws primarily upon the power-dependency work of Emerson (1962) to show how *both* power and dependency exchanges made the Nampa situation far more than the "flattening of an organization structure." Emerson adopts the intriguing view that for Party A (e.g., an individual, group, nation, etc.) to have power, it must have power over others (e.g., Party B). Therefore, B must be dependent upon A to the extent that it values goals that are mediated by A, particularly when there is no outside access to these same goals. In other words, B's dependence provides the basis for A's power, and the power of A over B is equal to and based upon the dependence of B upon A.

The third premise tends to combine aspects of the first two by assuming that Dr. West sought to increase mutual dependency within and beyond Nampa in order to expand mutual as well as individual power. The assumption has been well stated by Thompson (1967) who notes that:

> Finally, the power-dependence concept advanced here provides an important escape from the zero-sum concept of power (Emerson, 1962; Parsons, 1960), which assumes that in a system composed of A and B, the power of A is power at the expense of B. By considering power in the context of interdependence, we admit the possibility of A and B becoming increasingly powerful with regard to each other — the possibility that increasing interdependence may result in increased net power.

These then are the cornerstones of this chapter's point of view. Mixed systems, power-dependency, and their joint relevance to Nampa are the foci. Manifest goals, nonzero-sum assumptions, open systems, and rational organization planning are the concepts to be balanced against much of the earlier conceptual material. Our belief is that the resulting syntheses (e.g., mixed systems and power-dependency) provide a useful way of looking at the Nampa situation, at the history of organizational theory (e.g., we would modify Chapter VI statements by suggesting that *both* classical theory and human relations theory were prescriptive; the second served as an antithesis for the first), and at the whole issue of power and authority in organizations.

SOME FURTHER NOTES ON MIXED SYSTEMS

As stated above, we assume that managers are governed by both zero-sum and non-zero-sum rules; that latent assumptions and manifest goals are both important, particularly when the goals become self-fulfilling vehicles for the assumptions; and that managers lean upon both rational evidence and rationalization to guide their structuring of organizations. Some of this rational evidence is in the form of research on organizational design upon which either Dr. West or any other manager could rely. Briefly:

1. A series of experiments on communications networks (Leavitt, 1958; Glanzer and Glaser, 1961) showed that certain network designs worked "best" for certain goals and tasks. A highly centralized network generated highest productivity on highly routinized tasks. More egalitarian, decentralized networks generated higher creativity, more flexible problem solving, and higher morale, particularly with nonroutine tasks. These researches suggest that communications structures optimally vary with the nature of the task. Leavitt (1962) suggests that managers interpret those findings as a need for appropriate "differentiation" within organizations: for example, while creative research groups are freed up to create, the routine order clerks may be more tightly controlled by a computer control system. Guided by this research, a development center manager like Dr. West would differentiate his organization in the direction of colleague influence and project-centered responsibility — much as Dr. West attempted to do.

2. The notion of structure according to task is given further support by Woodward (1958) who compared the production organizations of 100 English companies. She found that the flattest organization structures and the lowest manager-to-worker ratios were in those firms with the lowest predictability of production techniques. In other words, task uncertainty tended to correlate with flattened structures; task certainty with more hierarchical structures.

3. Another study (Burns and Stalker, 1961) of 20 indus-

trial firms in the United Kingdom showed findings consistent with those cited above. Firms with more routine tasks and environments tended to be most highly structured with decisions made at higher levels. Those with less task certainty and lower environmental stability tended to be more organically structured. In the more organic companies, Burns and Stalker found more egalitarian communication patterns, even among hierarchical levels.

4. A study of production, sales, and research departments in six companies by Lawrence and Lorsch (1967) showed the importance of both differentiating and integrating structures and procedures. The high performing organizations tended to show greatest differentiation between production, sales, and research departments in: (a) structure, (b) interpersonal orientation, (c) time orientation, and (d) goal orientation. Research units, for example, tended to be: (a) least formally structured, (b) moderate to low in interpersonal orientation (depending upon whether the research was applied or fundamental), (c) longest on time orientation, and (d) most science-value oriented. However, the high performing organizations also had the strongest integrative links between departments. Lawrence and Lorsch suggest that the key to achieving *both* high differentiation and high integration lies in the conflict resolution patterns established between highly differentiated units.

In general, these findings show a high correlation between task-environmental uncertainty and (a) flatter organizational structures, (b) colleague-type communications patterns, (c) organic systems, (d) higher interaction patterns, and (e) lower level decision making. None of the studies cited above, or others like them (e.g., Udy, 1964; Bell, 1967; Blau, 1967; or Fouraker, manu.), tries to deny man's nonrational qualities. However, the findings suggest the importance of also taking rational consistencies into account. As best we can tell, Dr.

West did this in setting his manifest goals for the Nampa Center. The research evidence also suggests that there is cumulative rational evidence for organizational planners to use in organizational design. To believe this, and to use research as rational evidence, is to remove organizational structuring from the rationalization-only category to which it was consigned in the previous chapter.

Finally, in this section of the chapter, we wish to address the question of power expansion in a mixed system where both zero-sum and non-zero-sum rules operate. Dr. West seemed to assume that increases in total power for all groups were both possible and desirable. Other managers presumably made different and opposite assumptions. The Nampa study can be viewed as a situation where two kinds of power expansion could occur. The first involved external expansion of power into a receptive environment. It was best typified by Dr. West and the Junior Managers' increased influence over other CAPS members, the Sales Vice President, the Research Director, and Norfleet's R & D Vice President. The second form of power expansion occurred within Nampa. It involved increased interdependence such as developed between the Junior Managers and the Senior Scientists. Similar mutual power expansion seemed to develop between some Junior Managers and their Junior Scientist subordinates. Each gained more control over the other than they had previously had.

Other Junior Scientists, however, apparently did not gain the power they had expected. They may not have actually lost power, but their expectations of increased involvement, interdependence, and influence were not realized. They signaled their disenchantment with the CAPS program by indicating that their jobs had not been affected. Psychologically, they had lost power in terms of their expectations.

These examples of power expansion or contraction (actual or psychological) would tend to occur under open system conditions where people assumed non-zero-sum rules; that is, they assumed that power could expand or contract for all parties mutually. However, what of closed system conditions where the assumed rules were more zero-sum? We need to examine the power problem in terms of relative as well as total power — in terms of ratios as well as absolute quantities.

If one party's power, for example, increases considerably in an organization, this may be experienced as a proportionate loss by others who see themselves on parallel tracks unless (a) they experience equal power increases or (b) they see alternative ways of meeting the same goals (at which time the system becomes more open). A person's power may increase, but if that of his fellows increases even more, he will experience a relative loss. Although an organization's total power may be nonfinite in theory, the component percentages still add up to a closed system of 100%. Particularly under competitive conditions, one tends to think in terms of comparative gains, share of market, relative power, and one party's gains being at the expense of another.

Under the Nampa Center conditions, the Senior Managers were most likely to experience the zero-sum rules. Both their superior, Dr. West, and their subordinates, the Junior Managers, had become less dependent upon them. Comparatively speaking, the Senior Managers lost power although it was anticipated by Dr. West that this would be offset by gains resulting from long-range planning. According to our interpretative scheme, that source of gain remained unrealized, not because of an inevitably closed system, but because no basis was established upon which a new mutual dependency system with outside units could be built. They had no power-dependency base upon which to build.

This brings us closer to the critical relationships between power and authority and power and dependency. From our point of view, again different from that expressed in Chapter

VI, authority is one form of power. Power represents a more general form of potential influence whose inital basis probably consisted of physical coercion being used to acquire property in the form of land and slaves. Those who possessed either of these had power; those who sought to possess them were the power seekers. As the history of man unfolded, other sources of power developed. Those without property sought power through such sources as the acquisition of knowledge or artistic achievement. Today, the more basic value sources of power seem to have phased into such qualities as hierarchical position, money, experience, specialized knowledge, personal effort, personal attractiveness, age, etc. (French and Raven, 1959; Landsberger, 1961; Mechanic, 1962; Katz and Kahn, 1966). Only when these sources are turned into power-dependency relationships, as we shall discuss in the next section, do they become candidates for more formalized authority. Authority, then, involves dependencies which are (a) collectively accepted by those in the more dependent position and (b) defined into prescribed and accepted roles. This formalization or institutionalization process is seen most clearly in the form of positional authority. The more dependent subordinate has accepted his dependency and the defined role prescriptions in the name of custom, tradition, efficiency, and the like. A similar form of conversion from power-dependency-to-authority has more recently occurred using knowledge as the power source. The authority of knowledge, or professional authority, has become institutionalized in universities and scientific R & D centers. Those with one type of specialized knowledge accept their specialized roles and their dependency upon those with other types of specialized knowledge.

Superficially, both power and authority seem very different from dependency. Mutual dependence seems very unlike mutual power. Power increases seem unrelated to dependency increases. Nevertheless, the two issues are strongly related. Dependency is "the other side" of the power coin, and the one could not exist without the other.

Some Notes on Power and Dependency

Emerson's model of power (1962) suggests that power is a vacant concept unless we specify "power over whom." This means that power is an attribute of a social relation, not, as Chapter III implies, something that "individuals take within themselves or make internal." The social relationship involves each party being dependent upon others for goal achievement as well as influential over the goals of other parties. For example, thinking momentarily of only the Junior Managers (jm) and the Senior Managers (sm), we could set up two equations:

(1) The power of the Senior Managers over the Junior Managers is equal to and based upon the dependençe of the Junior Managers upon the Senior Managers, or $Psm/jm = Djm/sm$.

(2) The power of the Junior Managers over the Senior Managers is equal to and based upon the dependence of the Senior Managers upon the Junior Managers, or $Pjm/sm = Dsm/jm$.

By bringing the two equations together as shown below, we can see how both power and dependency can become mutual or interdependent characteristics. Equation A shows a balanced relationship. Equation B shows an unbalanced relationship.

<table>
<tr><td align="center">*Equation A*
Balanced Relationship</td><td align="center">*Equation B*
Unbalanced Relationship</td></tr>
<tr><td align="center">$Psm/jm = Djm/sm$
$\parallel \qquad \parallel$
$Pjm/sm = Dsm/jm$</td><td align="center">$Psm/jm = Djm/sm$
$\vee \qquad \vee$
$Pjm/sm = Dsm/jm$</td></tr>
</table>

Emerson adopts the position that an unbalanced relationship tends to encourage either rationalization or balancing

on the dependent party's part. Rationalization serves to make
dependency palatable and acceptable. It reduces the pains in-
curred in being dependent upon a more powerful other party.
It also tends to legitimatize the unbalanced power-dependency
relationship. When accompanied by role expectations and
prescriptions (e.g., father, boss, teacher), rationalization serves
as a basis for establishing and perpetuating formal authority
(i.e., legitimated power) relationships. In Nampa, as in all
formal organizations, the combination of subordinate rationalization and member role prescriptions were two major
qualities that defined the formal organization structure. In
this sense, formal authority is derived from power-dependency relationships as well as vice versa.

Balancing of the power-dependency relationship, on the
other hand, differs from rationalization in that it alters
rather than accepts the existing power ratios. In this sense,
Dr. West not only sought to increase Nampa's total power;
he also tried to make Junior Managers and technical people
less dependent upon their superiors in the hierarchy. He
talked about having more decisions made on the basis of
knowledge and fewer made on the basis of position. In effect,
Dr. West's program aimed at new balances through the increasing or decreasing of dependencies. In addition, he sought
to develop new and multiple dependencies which could
become mutual power-dependency relationships. Thus, the
dependency of Junior Managers upon Senior Managers was
reduced; at the same time, their total dependency (and
power) was increased *vis à vis* the CAPS members, Dr. West,
the Senior Scientists, and outside sources.

Emerson (1962) suggests four ways in which power-dependency relationships are balanced. Each will be described below with some illustrative evidence from the Nampa study.

1. The more dependent party can reduce its motivational
investment in goals mediated by the more powerful party.
This can mean abandonment, withdrawal, or reduction of

these goals. It means a denial of dependency by the more dependent party. In Nampa, this kind of withdrawal seems most evident among the CAPS Junior Scientists and the Non-CAPS Senior Scientists (Figure 15). Both groups showed an increasing willingness to consider outside job offers at the same level. It seems likely that such anticipatory withdrawal was one way the scientist groups had of shifting dependency from Nampa to other sources. A similar but less mobile pattern is often seen among blue collar production workers who withdraw from dependency upon management. They implicitly reject goals of production and wage increases in favor of production restrictions, informal conformity, and so forth.

2. The more dependent party can build new dependency relationships beyond the more powerful party. This involves the expansion and diffusion of dependency, presumably with the expectation that the new network of power-dependency relationships will be more balanced than the old. This is, in effect, what happened to the Junior Managers and CAPS Senior Scientists. Each group was able to build a new set of dependency relationships (a) with outside groups and (b) with each other. In each case, the exchange system that developed showed more mutual power-dependency characteristics than the old ones that each had had with the Senior Managers or outsiders.

3. The more powerful party can increase its motivational investment in goals mediated by the more dependent party. This kind of increased dependency by the superior upon subordinates occurred in Nampa when Dr. West focused attention and resources upon the technical projects under the Junior Managers. Prior to this time, technical projects had been subordinated to the larger and more glamorous Filtron Project. Dr. West's announced dependency on the Junior Managers increased their power over him to the same extent that he felt dependency. By the same token, Junior Managers

were dependent upon Dr. West for maintaining much of their newfound power and autonomy.

4. The more powerful party may fail to find other ways of reaching goals except through the more dependent party. This often comes from knowing or unknowing coalitions being formed which include the more dependent party. In the Nampa case, Junior Managers formed a *de facto* coalition as suggested in prior chapters. However, the coalition included not only Dr. West and the Senior Scientists, but other outsiders (e.g., CAPS members, Dr. West's superior in Norfleet, other members of the Marketing and Research Departments). This served to make the Senior Managers more dependent upon the Junior Managers than they had been and helped to balance the power-dependency relationship.

These four balancing approaches can apply in hierarchical, diagonal, or lateral relationships. For illustrative purposes above, we tended to concentrate on power-dependency in hierarchical relationships. However, the same processes could apply in other organizational relationships (e.g., staff-line, peer group, interdepartmental). We shall discuss several of these in the next section on how power-dependency seemed to work in Nampa's mixed system. By way of review, though, we might summarize here by noting that unbalanced relationships lend themselves to five adjustment processes. These may be summarized as:

1. Acceptance of dependency by those placed in the more dependent position.

2. Reduced dependency or withdrawal by the more dependent party.

3. Diffusion of dependency onto other objects by the more dependent party.

4. Dependency increases initiated by the more powerful party.

5. Blockage of alternate dependencies sought by the more powerful party.

With these in mind, and with a focus that now includes dependency as well as power, we can move on to the final section of this chapter. This section examines Dr. West's attempts to increase mutual dependency and power within and beyond Nampa.

Nampa's Mixed System and the Attempts to Increase Mutual Power-Dependency

The reader should note that the section heading contains implicitly several of the assumptions discussed earlier in the chapter. Since they are important assumptions, we shall review them briefly before going on. In essence:

The Nampa Center was a complex combination of closed and open systems. We refer to it as a mixed system in which both zero-sum and non-zero-sum assumptions prevailed. Dr. West attempted to design an organization in which both total power-dependency and relative power-dependency changed. His emphasis, though, seems to have been on increasing Nampa's overall power-dependency. These attempted increases relied upon one or more balancing operations. The balancing operations served either as efforts to expand mutual power-dependency relationships outside of Nampa or as efforts to increase the level of power-dependence mutuality among Nampa's members.

The findings suggest, at least during the period observed, that Dr. West was overly optimistic in hoping that all parties could gain power and prestige. Some would also accuse him of unrealistically trying to increase professional authority without expecting it to be at the expense of positional authority. Yet research findings persistently assure us that the two are not necessarily incompatible (Barnes, 1960; Blau, 1968). Concluding another recent study, Hall (1968) observed:

> An assumption of interest conflict between the professional or the professional group and the employing organization appears to be unwarranted. If it is present, the bases of conflict in terms of professional attitudes and/or organizational structure should be made explicit.

In this case, we find it difficult in Nampa to find these bases of conflict in any overall fashion.

Instead, it appears that Dr. West and those over him used positional authority to open a new environmental door for Nampa's members. As Chapter V indicates, the conditions were ripe. Some tension existed in the environment; the large Filtron Project had been sold off, and there were no key development projects ready to take its place. Furthermore, Norfleet's new R & D vice president wanted to improve Norfleet's competitive position. He thought this could be done through more effective integrative work between the central Research Division, the Nampa Center, and the Westwood Marketing Division. In effect, he helped Dr. West to build a balanced power-dependency relationship among these three units. He also helped Dr. West to establish exchange relationships with the Research Director, the Sales Vice President, and himself. The nature of these boss and colleague exchanges brought both greater dependency and greater power to Dr. West as a result of a balancing process using dependency diffusion. Though Dr. West was probably even more dependent upon his own boss (for active support as well as judgment), he now had a wider network of power-dependency. From this initial situation, there emerged the CAPS committees involving project members from Research and Sales working with Nampa personnel.

The pattern continued to expand. The Senior Scientists and some Junior Scientists joined Junior Managers in the lateral-diagonal exchanges. The expanded power-dependency system moved into Nampa's environment. The Junior Managers and Senior Scientists, along with Dr. West, established new power-dependency exchanges, partly at the expense of the Senior Managers whose search for alternate goal paths had been blocked.

The Senior Managers and the Director failed to establish an environmental set of mutual dependencies for the Senior Managers. Such exchanges were needed if the Senior Managers were to have an influence over the long-range plans of the Westwood Division, but they were not forthcoming. Consequently, with the Junior Managers, the Senior Scientists, and the Director all growing less dependent on them, the Senior Managers experienced a loss in power and found themselves even more dependent upon the Director than before. As was pointed out in Chapter II, this matched their expectations, and they rationalized the power loss and the increased dependency during this period rather than attempting to reduce or diffuse the dependency through new exchange relationships. In effect, they assumed a closed system for themselves and perhaps rightly so. They perceived little chance to change their environment, possibly because their long-range planning directive may have threatened others in the Westwood Division already engaged in tentative planning. In retrospect, one can only speculate as to how the Senior Managers could have built stronger power-dependency exchanges with outside units in the Westwood Division, the Norfleet Company, or beyond (e.g., trade associations, universities, consultants).

For the Junior Scientists, there was a problem that was both similar and different. Unlike the Senior Managers, they tended to have high hopes and assumed an open system environment once the CAPS projects started. However, diffused dependencies never materialized for many of them. They remained dependent upon their Junior Manager bosses. This dependency was frustrating, because it was accompanied by decreases in contact between the two. Some Junior Managers also became less dependent upon their Junior Scientist subordinates, thus reducing the latter's power over their bosses. These Junior Scientists could see their own power reduced while their superiors had established outside dependencies and subsequent power relationships. The system became a closed one for these Junior Scientists, just as it had for the Senior Managers.

Other Junior Scientists, however, reported that their work had been positively affected by the CAPS project work. In these cases, it appears that two kinds of balancing occurred. First, Junior Managers initiated greater dependency upon subordinates for contribution, and involvement. This gave the subordinates greater power over their bosses and vice versa. Secondly, these same Junior Scientists seemed able to expand or diffuse their power-dependency relationships beyond the Junior Manager. Data from Chapter IV, as well as other research evidence (Pelz and Andrews, 1966), indicate that multiple dependencies correlate with high performance among scientists and engineers.

These findings give us some idea as to the conditions that make either total power or relative power most salient in a mixed open-closed system. Total power seemed most salient under conditions where each party could increase interparty dependencies as well as help diffuse the other party's dependencies. Some Junior Managers, for example, increased mutual dependency between themselves and their Junior Scientists while at the same time increasing the dependency contacts these Junior Scientists had with others. By contrast, relative power seemed most salient under those conditions where neither mutual nor multiple dependencies were strengthened or created. Although Dr. West hoped that Senior Managers and Junior Scientists could establish new exchanges with others inside and outside of Nampa, most did not. In each case, either they preferred not to enter another overdependent relationship or they could not find a sponsor to help expand their power-dependency relationships. Consequently, they remained dependent upon a superior who had become less dependent upon them and who did not, or could not, help them to create multiple dependencies. Without the new dependencies, they were unable to work toward an increased number of power-dependency exchanges. In each case, too, subordinates seemed caught up in a zero-sum game with their superiors. Without environmental outlets, each subordinate seemed to use his superior as a relative measure of his own power.

* * * * * *

These pages, then, represent an alternative point of view for the reader to consider. We began, as did Chapter VI, with the research and findings of this study as a base point for interpretation. However, our readings of the Nampa data and the field situation itself led to different interpretations from those expressed on some pages of this book and particularly in Chapter VI.

From our point of view, the complexities described in this chapter are critical in organizations. Beginning with an effort to examine antitheses as well as theses, we have tried to work toward a more synthesized point of view. As we understand the Nampa situation, Dr. West had rational as well as nonrational reasons for his particular organizational design. His manifest goals, as best we are able to determine from the data and from our knowledge of the man, were consistent with his more latent motives. Both placed great importance upon building Nampa's total power through increases in individual power. For the most part, Dr. West sought these power increases from units in a receptive environment. In this sense, Dr. West seemed to assume an open rather than a closed system and tried to set up non-zero-sum rules within the organization.

In trying to increase Nampa's total power, Dr. West also increased its multiple dependencies within and beyond

Nampa. In this chapter, this caused us to review and reinterpret the nature of power, authority, and dependence. In our view, power is the more basic dimension, but it cannot be considered apart from dependency; that is, the power of one party is equal to and based upon the dependence of the other party, and vice versa.

Consequently, this chapter raises a series of issues not examined directly in earlier chapters. We have stressed the dual importance of both open *and* closed systems, zero-sum *and* non-zero-sum rules, latent *and* manifest goals, rational *and* nonrational thinking, power *and* dependency, total power *and* relative power, organizational structure *and* exchange mechanisms, external power gains *and* internal power gains, limited dependencies *and* multiple dependencies, etc. The list seems long, but the principle is elementary. Organizational life, like other arenas of human activity, is a rich and complex phenomenon and is richer still in its possibilities. It seems least likely that we shall understand this richness if we arbitrarily choose one dimension or another as singularly relevant (e.g., manifest or latent, zero-sum or non-zero-sum).

Another point of view is reflected in this chapter. It presents a more complex, but in our view a more realistic, model of organizational life. It also encourages multidimensional exploration rather than premature explanation. For at this point in the study of organizations, little is to be gained by assuming that organizations are either open or closed while men's motives are either manifest or latent. The greater gains, it seems to us, will come from exploring the circumstances and ways under which either one or both exist. In this sense, exploration must accompany explanations of organizational behavior. In this sense, too, we have tried to keep the two processes in tune with each other in this chapter. Both were stressed rather than sacrificing one in order to emphasize the other, in the belief that man's quest for knowledge and effective action will thereby be optimized.

APPENDIX A

Questionnaire Items

THE WORDING of the written questions used in gathering the data analyzed in Chapter IV are presented below. They are reproduced here in the order in which the data from these questions were considered in Chapter IV. The table or figure in which the responses to a question are summarized is noted preceding each question. Questions used to gather data both before and after the changes are marked "comparative" while those asked only afterward are designated as "retrospective."

Table 1 (comparative)

How satisfied are you with the Development Center as a hard-hitting organization, capable of competing successfully with similar organizations in industry?

——— Very satisfied

——— Somewhat satisfied

——— Mildly dissatisfied

——— Very dissatisfied

Table 2 (retrospective)

Comparing the period since the introduction of the Project Groups and the CAPS Program to a similar period prior to September 1960, have you found yourself more involved in your work?

——— More

——— Less

——— No change

Table 3 (comparative)

If another organization were to offer you a position with just about the same formal responsibilities and rewards that you now have, how seriously would you consider changing organizations?

—— I would be very interested in such an offer and would definitely
        consider taking it.

—— I would be interested, and I might even take it.

—— I would be interested, but I don't think I would take it.

—— The offer wouldn't interest me at all.

Figure 6 (comparative)

How frequently do you contact each of these persons as a general
rule? (Check one in each column)

	Immediate Chief	*Person above Chief*
Several times a day	————————	————————
About once a day	————————	————————
Several times a week	————————	————————
Several times a month	————————	————————
Less often	————————	————————

Figure 7 (retrospective)

Comparing the period since the introduction of the Project Groups
and the CAPS Program to a similar period prior to September 1960,
have you had more autonomy than you had been previously given?

—— More

—— Less

—— No change

Figure 8 (retrospective)

Comparing the period since the introduction of the Project Groups
and the CAPS Program to a similar period prior to September 1960,
has your immediate chief apparently had more autonomy?

—— More

—— Less

—— No change

Table 4 (retrospective) (Also see question listed above for Figure 7)
In January 1961 the CAPS Program was formally instituted.

a. Have you since been a member of a CAPS Project?

———— Yes ———— No

b. Was your own work situation affected by this change?

———— Yes ———— No

Table 5A (retrospective)

Comparing the period since the introduction of the Project Groups and the CAPS Program to a similar period prior to September 1960, have the changes had a beneficial effect on the Center?

———— Beneficial

———— Detrimental

———— No change

Table 5B (retrospective)

During the last year and a half, a number of changes have been instituted in the organization of the Development Center. In your opinion which has there been? (check one)

———— Far too much change

———— Somewhat more change than necessary

———— Exactly the amount of needed change

———— Somewhat less change than necessary

———— Far too little change

Table 5C (retrospective)

In the future, at the Development Center, which would you like to see? (check one)

———— More frequent and rapid changes so we can keep up

———— Things continue at about the rate they have been

———— Less frequent and rapid changes so we can settle down and get something done

Figure 9 (retrospective)

Comparing the period since the introduction of the Project Groups and the CAPS Program to a similar period prior to September 1960, have you personally been more productive?

———— More

———— Less

———— No change

Figure 10 (retrospective)

Comparing the period since the introduction of the Project Groups and the CAPS Program to a similar period prior to September 1960, has your work group been more productive?

———— More

———— Less

———— No change

Figure 11 (See question listed under Table 1)

Figure 12 (See question listed under Table 2)

Figure 13 (retrospective)

Comparing the period since the introduction of the Project Groups and the CAPS Program to a similar period prior to September 1960, have you found your work more satisfying?

———— More

———— Less

———— No change

Figure 14 (comparative)

From your experience working under various people and your general experience with supervisors, on the whole how satisfied are you with your immediate chief?

———— Very satisfied

———— Somewhat satisfied

———— Mildly dissatisfied

———— Very dissatisfied

Figure 15 (See question listed under Table 3)

Table 6 (See questions listed under Figures 9, 10, Table 2, and Figure 13)

Table 7A (See question listed under Figure 14)

Table 7B (See question listed under Table 3)

Table 8 (comparative)

What are the actual and preferred relations between your chief and you, in determining what concrete *work problems or assignments* or follow-up steps you (or your staff) will work on next? (Assume that the general area of work has already been established.) In column A, rank the items according to what is actually the most typical or frequent, starting with "1"; in column B rank the methods as you would prefer them used, starting with "1" as the method most preferred.

In regard to work problems or assignments:	Column A *Actually Occurs*	Column B *Prefer to See Done*
(a) The chief talks the work over thoroughly with me, and gives considerable weight to my views when he makes the decisions.	——	——
(b) The chief examines the work to date and he himself makes whatever decisions or recommendations he feels are best.	——	——
(c) The chief talks it over with me (and perhaps with other people working on these problems) and we jointly formulate the decisions or recommendations.	——	——
(d) Such decisions or recommendations are up to me (or my staff); my chief simply gives routine approval.	——	——

Table 9

One form of the California F-Scale was completed by all the respondents in this study. Although these data were collected for another research study, they were used here to test alternative explanations of the study's findings. The form of the F-Scale (which we entitled the Personal Opinion Survey) is reproduced below.

Personal Opinion Survey

The statements on the following pages are concerned with opinions on important social questions. Each statement is an opinion which you may have thought about, read about, or heard others talking about. We are interested in learning how much you agree or disagree with each of the 24 statements.

The statements represent many different points of view, some of which you may agree with and others with which you may disagree. You will see that they cover kinds of ideas about which people may have differing opinions. Therefore, this is not a test of intelligence or knowledge. The best answer for you is how much you personally agree or disagree with each statement.

Please read each statement carefully and indicate in the space provided how much you agree or disagree with it by marking the space alongside the statement according to the following scale:

Agree strongly	+3
Agree moderately	+2
Agree slightly	+1
Disagree slightly	−1
Disagree moderately	−2
Disagree strongly	−3

For your convenience, this scale will be repeated at the top of each page. Please answer every question, indicating your own personal point of view. We think you will find some interesting ideas presented in the statements. It should take you less than five minutes to complete this series of questions.

Please indicate your agreement or disagreement with each of the following statements by writing a number from −3 to +3 in the space provided according to the following scale:

Disagree strongly	−3	Agree strongly	+3
Disagree moderately	−2	Agree moderately	+2
Disagree slightly	−1	Agree slightly	+1

---

1. ———— Most of our social problems would be solved if we could somehow get rid of the immoral, crooked, and feebleminded people.

2. ———— No weakness or difficulty can hold us back if we have enough will power.

3. ———— Young people sometimes get rebellious ideas, but as they grow up, they ought to get over them and settle down.

4. ———— If people would talk less and work more, everybody would be better off.

5. ———— What the youth needs most is strict discipline, rugged determination, and the will to work and fight for family and country.

6. ———— The wild sex of the old Greeks and Romans was tame compared to some of the goings-on in this country, even in places where people might least expect it.

7. ———— When a person has a problem or worry, it is best for him not to think about it, but to keep busy with more cheerful things.

8. ———— An insult to our honor should always be punished.

9. ———— No sane, normal, decent person could ever think of hurting a close friend or relative.

10. ———— Homosexuals are hardly better than criminals and ought to be severely punished.

11. ———— Nowadays when so many different kinds of people move around and mix together so much, a person has to protect himself especially carefully against catching an infection or disease from them.

12. ———— Most people don't realize how much our lives are controlled by plots hatched in secret places.

Please indicate your agreement or disagreement with each of the following statements by writing a number from −3 to +3 in the space provided according to the following scale:

Disagree strongly	−3	Agree strongly	+3
Disagree moderately	−2	Agree moderately	+2
Disagree slightly	−1	Agree slightly	+1

---

13. —— What this country needs most, more than laws and political programs, is a few courageous, tireless, devoted leaders in whom the public can put their faith.

14. —— Some people are born with an urge to jump from high places.

15. —— People can be divided into two distinct classes: the weak and the strong.

16. —— There is hardly anything lower than a person who does not feel a great love, gratitude, and respect for his parents.

17. —— Every person should have complete faith in some supernatural power whose decisions he obeys without question.

18. —— Some day it will probably be shown that astrology can explain a lot of things.

19. —— Familiarity breeds contempt.

20. —— Sex crimes, such as rape and attacks on children, deserve more than mere imprisonment; such criminals ought to be publicly whipped, or worse.

21. —— Obedience and respect for authority are the most important virtues children should learn.

22. —— Nowadays, more and more people are prying into matters that should remain personal and private.

23. —— Science has its place, but there are many important things that can never possibly be understood by the human mind.

24. —— Human nature being what it is, there will always be war and conflict.

The Concept of Authority and Organizational Change

THE STRATEGIC importance of the authority system as both a vehicle for change and a target for alteration in organizational change efforts is widely recognized. Yet an understanding of the role authority plays in change efforts remains elusive. Few words have greater currency in organizational theory and in organizational life than does the term authority. Still the concept of authority is as open to conflicting interpretations as any in the literature on organizations and nowhere does the confusion seem so great as in the discussions of organizational change. The following discussion attempts to trace the roots of the ambiguity surrounding authority as a concept and its usages in two ways. First, some of the pertinent historical issues in the development of the concept of authority are reviewed. Second, some of the major approaches to organizational change over recent decades are examined in terms of their impact on the authority system.

THE CONCEPT OF AUTHORITY

If laymen have trouble finding common ground when they try to discuss authority, they can at least take comfort in the fact that social scientists and organizational theorists have had similar difficulty wrestling with the same thorny problem. Every few years a writer will ruefully agree with earlier writers that authority remains a difficult concept on which to establish any agreement in terms. For example, note Peabody's comment in 1962:

> Despite numerous attempts at conceptual clarification and a growing body of empirical inquiries focusing on organizational behavior, Herbert A. Simon could conclude in 1957 that "there is no consensus in management literature as to how the term authority should be used." [1]

Historically, the roots of this problem go deep. The classical pattern of authority pictures a hierarchical authority figure who rules some form of organization, be it family, clan, tribe, or kingdom. Tradition has it that this figure's word was law. But as Rubenstein and Haberstroh (1960) note:

> This organizational system existed less in practice than in theory. Even in ancient times subordinates were able to arrange some form of protection for themselves against the caprice of their ruler, and democratic forms also appeared very early in history.[2]

Then, as now, subordinates held some recognized ability to influence each other as well as their superiors. This fact has continued to raise a fundamental question. Should the term authority refer only to the ability to influence which derives from hierarchical position, or should it also include that which derives from other sources as well? This seemingly simple question has assumed major theoretical importance over the years. Both schools of thought are represented in formal theories of organization. The concept of hierarchical authority was designed into a theory of bureaucracy [3] by Max Weber (1864–1920), a German historian turned sociologist. A more inclusive theory of authority was set forth by Chester I. Barnard (1886–1961), an American industrialist turned theorist.[4] Weber drew his theory of bureaucracy from observations of church, military, and political life in Europe during the early 20th century. Barnard drew upon his 30 years as an industrialist and related this to the social system concepts of L. J. Henderson, a Harvard biochemist turned sociologist, and Henderson's associate, Elton Mayo. Mayo and Henderson in turn took some of their concepts from the Italian sociologist, Vilfredo Pareto (1848–1923).[5]

The differences between these two positions have widened over the years as the followers of each position have multiplied. In 1961, Hopkins criticized the existing gap but nevertheless noted:

> Organizational theory today contains two different views of systems of bureaucratic authority. In one, which has its source in the writings of Max Weber, they are power structures operating in quasi-judicial fashion: rational values legitimate them, trained experts

run them, and the principle of hierarchy, prescribing a positive relation between the rank of a unit and its power, defines their shape. In the other, developed most fully by Chester I. Barnard, they are communications processes. Here they function to apprise decision makers of relevant matters of fact and to inform those who execute the decisions of their responsibilities. In this conception, neither legitimacy nor hierarchy plays a particularly central role. Both occur, but individual self-interests rather than shared moral commitments provide the main motivations, and the lateral extension of the system in physical space is more salient than its vertical extension in stratified social space. If the first view suggests the image of a pyramid, the second suggests a wheel, with the lines of communication as so many spokes radiating from the few persons at the organization's center who make the decisions to the many along the outer rim who finally carry the decisions out. In one, then, the outstanding elements are power, hierarchy, legitimacy; in the other, decision making, communication, and rational self-interest. Taken together, they comprise the major concepts currently used in the study of bureaucratic authority.[6]

Sources of Authority

Inevitably, there have been a number of attempts to subsume, reconcile, or cut across these two theories of authority. Most have found little support and have remained isolated intellectual ventures. One type of analysis has taken root, however, and has provided an area in which it has been possible to establish common points of agreement. This approach to the understanding of the concept seeks to examine authority in terms of the various sources or bases from which it derives. This is a notion which finds its roots in both Weber's and Barnard's work, but which has been developed beyond the manner in which it was used by either author.

Weber set the pattern for this type of analysis through his typology of three "pure types of legitimate authority": (a) Rational-Legal Authority — arising from the acceptance of a person's legally appointed position in the organization and his "right to issue commands"; (b) Traditional Authority — arising from traditional personal loyalties to a ruling family or clan; and (c) Charismatic Authority — arising from devotion to the exceptional sanctity, heroism, or exemplary character of an individual person.[7] It was part of Weber's main thesis that the first of these three, rational-legal authority, provides the basis for the highest degree of organizational efficiency and indeed, that the development of rational-legal authority had been identical with the development of the modern corporation.

The two elements which Weber combined in his view of rational-legal authority, however, were characterized by Barnard as separate and distinct. Without referring to Weber, Barnard divided authority in organizations between "authority of position" and "authority of leadership." By authority of position, Barnard meant the authority held by an individual by virtue of his formal position in the organizational hierarchy. By authority of leadership, he referred to that authority based on superior ability, knowledge, and understanding regardless of formal position.[8]

It has been on this point also that Weber's students have been his most severe critics. Parsons, in his English translation of Weber's work, first called attention to the fact that the "rational-legal" designation is internally inconsistent. Weber attached great importance to technical competence as a basis for efficient administration, and implicit in his scheme of bureaucratic administration is the assumption that hierarchical rank will coincide with technical competence and knowledge. Parsons noted that it is not logically necessary that someone holding a formal position in an organization should have either superior knowledge or superior skill as compared to those subject to his orders.[9] Later students of organizational life have not only followed Parsons in challenging the assumption that position-based and knowledge-based authority logically coincide, but have pointed to a fundamental tension between the two. Gouldner pointed out in 1959 that:

> . . . there are two fundamentally different criteria for the legitimation of authority — authority based on technical knowledge and experience, and authority based on incumbency in office — simultaneously operating in the same organization. One of the deepest tensions in the modern organization . . . derives from the divergence of these two bases of authority.[10]

Even more recently, Victor A. Thompson in a book entitled *Modern Organization* advanced the thesis that:

> . . . the most symptomatic characteristic of modern bureaucracy is the growing imbalance between ability and authority.[11]

Blau and Scott in their book on *Formal Organizations* even raise the question of a negative relationship between the two:

> Recent research that compares formal organizations in order to establish the empirical relations between their various characteristics also helps us to answer a question that has been repeatedly raised in this book and in the literature in general: namely, whether hierarchical bureaucratic authority and professional expertise tend to go together as Weber assumes, or whether they are alternative methods of administration and thus independent or perhaps even inversely related.[12]

These two sources of authority (formal position and recognized professional expertise) do not exhaust the list of bases on which authority is established and exercised in organization, but they clearly dominate in modern corporate life. A number of other authority bases have been identified, but they lack the salience and clarity of these two. We noted earlier Weber's designation of charismatic authority arising from the common devotion to some exceptional heroism or other attribute of an individual. Charismatic authority exists in modern organizations, but frequently, the organization will move to legitimate this authority by formalizing it. The hero who "saved the company" will be promoted, usually. "Traditional authority," based on extended family ties and loyalties to inherited "powers to govern," is becoming less salient in at least American organization. Several writers, including Peabody,[13] Presthus,[14] and Simons,[15] categorize another source of authority, the "authority of legitimacy," or a "generalized diffidence toward authority." However, the distinction between this and position-based authority is not clear. Peabody, drawing on prior authors' work, concluded that "authority of legitimacy is inextricably fused in reality with . . . authority of position." Both Bennis and Litvak, in their typologies of authority sources, place in a separate category authority based on effective "human relations" and the leader's "knowledge of

the human aspect of administration." [16] Robert Presthus refers
to this authority based on "rapport with subordinates" and "the
ability to mediate immediate individual needs." [17] However, the
attempt to designate the power accumulated by an individual
through a skillful handling of his interpersonal exchanges with
others as a form of authority puts an undue strain on the concept.

APPROACHES TO ORGANIZATIONAL CHANGE

The number of approaches to the introduction of change in
organizations is infinite and each will have some impact on the
authority system. It is possible, however, and useful to classify
the major approaches to organizational change in use over the
last several decades and examine their impact on authority. One
fruitful classification divides these approaches according to the
organizational variable most prominent in the change attempt.
Using such a classification, we shall briefly consider three approaches to organizational change and their effect on authority.
They focus on:

    (a) changes in the technology,
    (b) changes in shared norms and values, and
    (c) changes in formal organization structure.[18]

These three variables are by no means independent. The demands of a certain technology often necessitate accommodating
shifts in organizational structure. The emergence of certain
behavioral norms is influenced by the formal structure, and the
structure is often very much a reflection of the commonly held
norms and values. Ultimately any change in one is likely to
affect all three. In spite of the interdependence of these variables,
however, the three approaches which concentrate on one of these
variables differ rather strikingly. This difference can best be
noted by examining the approaches themselves.

Technological Approaches

Some of the major changes in the authority relationships in
work settings have been brought on by the introduction of new

technical methods of producing goods. This is vividly illustrated if we step back far enough historically to recall the shifts
away from the old master-apprentice system brought about by
the machinery of the Industrial Revolution. Prior to its introduction, the employer was the owner, teacher, and role-model
for a subordinate who would some day occupy the position of
his master. The introduction of machine-paced, low-skill work,
along with large multilevel organizational structure, profoundly
altered authority relations. This shift was later accentuated by
the advent of the moving assembly line, made famous by Henry
Ford. The significance of technology for authority patterns as
well as the social exchanges has been examined in this country
by Walker, Guest, and Turner [19] and in England by researchers
from Tavistock Institute who have come to conceptualize the
firm as a socio-technical system.[20]

A second type of technological change, focused more directly
on the authority dimension, is best represented historically by
Frederick Taylor and the scientific management movement.[21]
By creating a new technical skill — that of the industrial engineer, with his own set of tools (standards, piece rates, stop watches,
etc.) — Taylor effected a remarkable shift of authority patterns in
the factory. The industrial engineer, by virtue of an accepted
expertise, took over much of the planning function from the line
supervisor (as well as from the worker). The logics of work
simplification and time standards became a potent source of
authority on the factory floor. The first line supervisor, stripped
of nearly all opportunity to influence how the work was to be
done, lost much of the authority which had previously sprung
from his knowledge and skill acquired over the years.

The modern-day counterpart of this type of technological
change seems to be the introduction of operations research techniques. Again the approach is to separate out a set of planners
(working from a highly logicized framework) from those who
are to carry out the work. The effects which the introduction of
operations research are having on the authority structure have
yet to be systematically studied, but the striking parallels between OR and scientific management suggest that OR's impact
on authority relations may be similarly dramatic.

Value-Centered Approaches

As we pointed out earlier, authority in an organization provides a primary source of power. It is built on the basis of shared values and beliefs about what is correct, or at least acceptable, behavior for people in various positions in the organization. Some of these shared beliefs are taken from the larger culture; some have emerged within a particular organization as a resultant of past experiences in performing the organization's tasks. These beliefs and values provide the rationale for the formal organization, for job assignments, etc. They have also usually been translated into a set of norms for behavior informally enforced in the organization.

A second approach to organizational change, primarily advocated and practiced by behavioral scientists who often refer to themselves as change agents, seeks to bring about change in the organization by directly seeking to alter these norms and values. In the technological approaches the logics of efficiency and cost were advanced to support change; in this approach the logics advanced are those concerning human motivation and personal growth.

The early work in what came to be called the "human relations movement" called attention to the power of the informal system and to the "authority" of the informal as well as the formal leader.[22] Those who conducted some of these early studies centered their efforts, not on altering authority relationships, but on helping the manager to recognize and understand the complex set of forces at work on the behavior of his subordinates.[23] One of the ways in which it was suggested the manager gain information about these forces in his own department was by "listening" and trying to "understand the other person from his point of view."

Such "listening" was not a neutral act, however. It altered the relationship between the superior and subordinate (or seemed to, depending on whether the manager was using this as a gimmick). Enthusiasts of this approach soon carried it far beyond the thinking of the researchers whose studies they cited and began exhorting managers toward an egalitarian "group-centered leadership" or "employee-centered supervision." Training courses were set up to teach the supervisors (mostly foremen) to take into account the needs and feelings of his men as a means of "motivating" them. These courses were ostensibly aimed at developing human relations skills, but a new model for authority relationships was also being advanced which laid heavy stress on the value of "individual growth" and personal satisfaction. Organizations with traditional authority relationships were described as working at cross purposes with human development,[24] while the promise was held out that not only would the new model result in greater productivity but personal growth and satisfaction would also be maximized.

The supervisor's training course as an instrument of organizational change was brought sharply into question by a study of the results of a training program at International Harvester Company. The study showed that the effects of the training program stressing a human relations model were nullified by the effect of the behavior of the supervisor's own chief. If the supervisor's chief was high on "Initiating Structure" for his subordinates, the supervisor reverted to the same pattern.[25]

In recent years the advocates of training as an approach to organizational change have sought to correct the features of this approach which have most frequently been the targets of its critics. First, there has been an increasing tendency to define total organizational change as the objective. Instead of trying to alter the attitudes and values of selected supervisors, the thrust is to change those commonly held mores which concern "acceptable" and desired behavior in the organization. Training, therefore, is prescribed to cut across all levels of the organization.[26] Second, the attempt is made to start the training at the top of the organization and work down.* [27] Third, and perhaps

---

* Argyris (1962), after completing a training session with the top executives in a large corporation, cited his experience as proof for a need to begin there:

"One may conclude from this and other experiences that it would not be wise to start laboratory training in a given organizational unit at the middle or lower levels. One may imagine what would have happened if the control group (subordinates of the men in the top group) had gone first. The top would probably never have considered the program. . . . Unless the top

most important, under current change attempts conditions are created which require that the members of the organization work out *with one another* the changes that are to take place in their relationships. Members are brought together to examine their present relationships (and compare them against certain criteria) and jointly work out changes. The methodological tool used to set up these conditions is what has come to be known as "laboratory training." The most well-known example of laboratory training is the "T Group," but there are also other variants. The central notion of using T-Group training is that participants are forced by the ambiguity of the situation, by the absence of legitimate external topics of discussion, and by the imperative of the Trainer to examine their own interpersonal relationships — the "here and now." [28] The apparent absence of structure pushes the participants toward defining and seeking joint solutions to their interpersonal problems in the group and to relate these to their back-home work relationships. The ambiguity of the laboratory setting and the sometimes jolting feedback have the purpose of "unfreezing" old relationships and authority patterns.

The "working out" of new relationships is the responsibility of the members of the organization, but the "change agents" are not indifferent as to the direction in which the authority patterns are shifted. As Leavitt points out, the "theoretical underpinnings, the prevalent values and the initial research results" of those who use this approach to change all point in the direction of "power equalization rather than power differentiation." [29] (Using our definition, the major attack is on the positional authority system.) An examination of the statements of the advocates of this approach make this point clear. Shepard and Blake point out that laboratory training is only a tool in an over-all program which is aimed at creating an "organic system" based on "mutual confidence and trust among members of the organization rather than authority-obedience relationships." A "wide sharing of control and responsibility" was cited as one of their objectives.[30] A

---

could be influenced, changes made at the middle or lower levels could create even greater problems and at the best would remain incapsulated in that particular unit."

training director in a west coast corporation utilizing T-Groups as a part of an organization development program set as one of their objectives the development of "norms within the organization that support open, direct confrontation of conflict (resolution of conflict without having to resort to the power structure)." Argyris states that the training experience (given to the top executives of a large organizational division) was aimed at replacing their "old" authoritarian values with "new" values.[31]

The methods used to achieve "power equalization" vary, of course. For example, Blake and his associates have developed a normative model of managerial behavior, and group relationships called the managerial grid, against which the members of the organization can compare their own relationships and which they can use as a model.[32] Others are quick to point out they have no such model as the grid. But even those change agents who do not advocate a specific normative model as Blake does make it clear through their behavior and their training designs that one of their major targets for change is the authority relationship. The T-group itself is a power-equalizing device in which status and roles brought into the group are de-emphasized and made illegitimate. The trainer of the T-Group, or "cluster" as it is now sometimes called, provides a role model who deliberately attempts to divest himself of positional authority and seeks a place in the group differentiated from other members only by the "resources" he can provide as a professional expert.

The effects of these recent attempts at organizational change utilizing laboratory training methods have yet to be determined. Some advocates claim that the pitfalls of the early human relations training courses have been avoided and that the changes being introduced are more likely to be more permanent. Unfortunately, there have been few systematic studies reporting the nature and the duration of the changes which are being introduced by this approach.

Structural Approaches

Probably the approach most commonly used to alter authority patterns is the structural approach. Paradoxically, this is also probably the approach about which we have the least empirical

data. The early writings in structural planning and change
tended to be more proscriptive than descriptive. Principles were
developed such as delegation of authority and assignment of responsibility, but as principles they were more likely to be ex-
pounded than used as variables in research. Some of the same
assumptions about a unidimensional rational-legal authority seen
in Weber's work were present in these writings. Authority was
primarily seen only as positional authority. Where such authority was not accepted, stronger leadership and discipline were
called for. Change attempts were most often a "clarification" of
areas of authority and responsibility.

One prevalent approach to the use of structure in changing
authority relationships has been characterized by the trend toward
decentralization and the establishment of profit centers. The
rapid growth of national and international corporations and the
consequent difficulties of transmitting the necessary information
throughout this complex system encouraged this trend. Along
with this came the difficulties of taking the multitude of differential local factors into account in decision making and the desire to measure small unit performances. All these factors pushed
this trend forward, although a number of management problems
were raised in applying the idea.[33] The computer, however, a
technological innovation, has raised into question and may be
reversing the trend toward decentralization and authority dis-
persion in large corporations.[34]

Research on the impact of the informal system in an organization, on emergent interpersonal relations, and on individual
motivation for many years obscured structure as a primary change
variable, at least in management literature. This research pointed
out the naiveté of some of the early structural approaches to
change. On the other hand, studies such as the one reported by
Worthy in 1950 rekindled an interest in structure as a potent influence on superior-subordinate relations. Worthy, reporting a
study done by the personnel department of Sears, Roebuck and
Co., found that the number of hierarchical levels in a store and
consequently the number of people reporting to a superior were
significantly related to the number of promotable subordinates
developed, as well as to store profitability.[35] Some writers have

criticized Worthy's generalizations as oversimplified,[36] but his study helped raise renewed interest in the strategic importance of the structural variable.

Some current students of organizational change place strong emphasis on formal structure, management controls, and work flows as largely determining the behavior of the manager in his relations with others. Sayles, for example, claims that a manager's relationships are in large part a function of these structural factors:

> Given the division of labor characteristic of modern public and private organizations, the number of special interests and viewpoints represented in diverse groups whose efforts must be coordinated, the inevitable conflicts and incompatibilities among various control measures, and the dynamic shifts in structures and pressures, the manager cannot pick and choose his style with impunity. His managerial behavior is a function of the organization of work and the controls operating on him (rewards and punishments). He must adopt a variety of administrative patterns to fit the varying requirements of the interface: where his job meets others.[37]

Recent empirical studies of structurally initiated change in authority relationships are of several kinds. A large part of the empirical studies on the effect of organizational structure, such as the Worthy study, tend to be laterally comparative rather than studies of change within the same organization.[38]

A second type of study examines the changing of authority relationships within one organization and the effects of these changes over a period of time, but without differentiating between the bases on which authority is established. Examples of this type of study would include Brown and Shepard's study of organizational change in a research laboratory [39] and Guest's study of successful change in an automobile assembly plant.[40] Guest's study might also be categorized as a study in management succession in which the authority structure was varied as a consequence of new management.

Only a few organizational changes fall into a third category, those which examine the struggle between the systems of position-based and knowledge-based authority. Although each uses a somewhat different language system from the one used here, three very interesting studies might be included: Jaques' *The Changing Culture of a Factory*,[41] McCleery's study of the warden's efforts to change authority patterns in the Oahu prison,[42] and Lawrence's study of behavior change in a supermarket chain.[43] Two common features should be noted in these instances of structural change. First, most were initiated by management rather than by outside agents. Second, in most cases they were consciously planned changes rather than changes almost completely imposed as were many of the technological changes. It is these two features which point up the need for an increased understanding of the problems and dynamics of this approach to organizational change, for the accessibility of structural change as a tool of line managers and its seeming susceptibility to rationalistic planning are likely to assure that the greatest part of deliberate change will continue to be initially structural in nature.

Reference Footnotes

(See Bibliography for publishing data)

CHAPTER III

1 Blau and Scott, *Formal Organizations*, pp. 27–30.
2 Hodgson, Levinson, and Zaleznik, *The Executive Role Constellation*, pp. 230–245.
3 Neustadt, *Presidential Power*.
4 Issues of morality and power are discussed in Selekman and Selekman, *Power and Morality in a Business Society*. See also Selekman, *A Moral Philosophy for Management*, pp. 100–108.
5 Tannenbaum, "The Concept of Organizational Control"; idem, "Control and Effectiveness in a Voluntary Organization"; Tannenbaum and Georgopoulos, "The Distribution of Control in Formal Organizations."
6 For discussion of rationality in organizations from the standpoint of decision making, see March and Simon, *Organizations*, pp. 136–171.

CHAPTER IV

1 Roethlisberger and Dickson, *Management and the Worker*.
2 Vroom, *Some Personality Determinants in the Effects of Participation*.

CHAPTER V

1 Guest, *Organizational Change*, pp. 17–39.
2 Seashore and Bower, *Changing the Structure and Functioning of an Organization*, p. 11.
3 Jaques, *The Changing Culture of a Factory*, pp. 45–48.
4 *Ibid.*, p. 310.
5 Blake, Mouton, Barnes, and Greiner, "Breakthrough in Organizational Development."
6 Greiner, "Antecedents of Planned Organizational Change," p. 62.
7 Guest, *op. cit.*, pp. 42 and 108.
8 Pelz, "Influence: A Key to Effective Leadership in the First-Line Supervisor."
9 Jaques, *op. cit.*, pp. 1–23.
10 Seashore and Bower, *op. cit.*, pp. 10–15.
11 Blake et al., *op. cit.*, p. 146.
12 Hovland, Janis, and Kelley, *Communication and Persuasion: Psychological Studies of Opinion Change*.
13 Mace, "Satisfaction in Work," pp. 5–12.
14 Loomis, "Tentative Types of Directed Social Change Involving Systematic Linkage."
15 Guest, *op. cit.*, pp. 40–53.
16 Jaques, *op. cit.*
17 Seashore and Bower, *op. cit.*, pp. 18, 26–45.

18 Blake et al., *op. cit.*, pp. 133–145.

19 Berelson and Steiner, *Human Behavior: An Inventory of Scientific Findings*, pp. 325–362.

20 Asch, "Effects of Group Pressure Upon the Modification and Distortion of Judgments," pp. 177–190.

21 Rice, *Productivity and Social Organizations: The Ahmedabad Experiment*, pp. 49–163.

22 Fleishman, Harris, and Burtt, *Leadership and Supervision in Industry*.

23 Blake et al., *op. cit.*, pp. 154, 155.

24 Guest, *op. cit.*, p. 45.

25 For a discussion of explicit confrontation as a vital function of the change agent's role, see Zaleznik and Moment, *The Dynamics of Interpersonal Behavior*, pp. 476–477.

26 Blake et al., *op. cit.*, p. 141.

27 Jaques, *op. cit.*, p. 306.

28 Guest, *op. cit.*, p. 42.

29 *Ibid.*, p. 60.

30 Blake et al., *op. cit.*, pp. 144–145.

31 Seashore and Bower, *op. cit.*, p. 53.

32 Roethlisberger and Dickson, *op. cit.*, p. 33.

33 National Research Council, *Fatigue of Workers: Its Relation to Industrial Production*, pp. 56–66.

34 Roethlisberger and Dickson, *op. cit.*, p. 33.

35 McClelland, "Toward a Theory of Motive Acquisition."

36 Seashore and Bower, *op. cit.*, pp. 11–12.

37 Blake et al., *op. cit.*, pp. 133–138, 441.

38 King and Janis, "Comparison of the Effectiveness of Improvised Versus Non-Improvised Role Playing in Producing Opinion Change," pp. 177–186.

CHAPTER VI

1 Herzberg et al., *Motivation to Work*.

2 Barnard, *The Functions of the Executive*, pp. 167–169.

3 Hodgson et al., *op. cit.*, p. 231 [italics added].

4 Rubenstein and Lasswell, *The Sharing of Power in a Psychiatric Hospital*. See p. 281 where similar interpretations are presented in an experiment on "flattening" the organization structure. Another case in point is presented in Jaques, *op. cit.*, and see also Strauss, "Some Notes on Power-Equalization."

5 March and Simon, *op. cit.*, Chapter II.

6 Homans, *Social Behavior: Its Elementary Forms*.

7 Barnard, *op. cit.*

8 Roethlisberger and Dickson, *op. cit.* Also White and Lippitt, "Leader Behavior and Membership Reaction in Three 'Social Climates'," pp. 585–611.

Reference Footnotes 215

9 Zaleznik, Christensen, and Roethlisberger, *The Motivation, Productivity, and Satisfaction of Workers.* Also Zaleznik, *Worker Satisfaction and Development.*

10 French and Coch, "Overcoming Resistance to Change," pp. 257–279.

11 Bradford, Gibb, and Benne, *T-Group Theory and Laboratory Method: Innovation in Re-education.*

12 McGregor, *The Human Side of Enterprise.*

13 Crozier, *The Bureaucratic Phenomenon.*

14 Blau, *The Dynamics of Bureaucracy.* Also Dalton, *Men Who Manage.*

CHAPTER VII

1 Tannenbaum, *Control in Organizations,* p. 14.

2 *Ibid.*

APPENDIX B

1 Peabody, "Perceptions of Organizational Authority."

2 Rubenstein and Haberstroh, eds., *Some Theories of Organization,* p. 61.

3 See Weber, *The Theory of Social and Economic Organization.*

4 Barnard, *The Functions of the Executive.*

5 Pareto, *The Mind and Society.* See also Henderson, *Pareto's General Sociology;* Mayo, *The Human Problems of an Industrial Civilization;* Roethlisberger and Dickson, *Management and the Worker.*

6 Hopkins, "Bureaucratic Authority: The Convergence of Weber and Barnard."

7 Weber, *op. cit.,* pp. 328–363.

8 Barnard, *op. cit.,* pp. 173–174.

9 Weber, *op. cit.,* pp. 58–60, ff. 4.

10 Gouldner, "Organizational Analysis," p. 413.

11 Thompson, *Modern Organization,* p. 6.

12 Blau and Scott, *Formal Organizations,* pp. 206–207.

13 Peabody, *op. cit.,* pp. 466–468.

14 Presthus, "Authority in Organizations," pp. 88–91.

15 Simon, "Authority."

16 Bennis, "Leadership Theory and Administrative Behavior: The Problem of Authority," and Litvak, "Models of Bureaucracy That Permit Conflict."

17 Presthus, *op. cit.,* pp. 88–91.

18 Our categorization of approaches to change was influenced by an article by Leavitt in *Handbook of Organizations.*

19 Walker, Guest, and Turner, *The Foreman on the Assembly Line.*

20 Miller, "Technology, Territory, and Time." Trist et al., *Organizational Choice.*

21 Taylor, *Scientific Management.*

22 Roethlisberger and Dickson, *op. cit.*

23 Roethlisberger, *Management and Morale.*

24 Argyris, *Personality and Organization.*

25 Fleishman, Harris, and Burtt, *Leadership and Supervision in Industry.*
26 Shepard and Blake, "Changing Behavior Through Cognitive Change."
   Blake, Mouton, Barnes, and Greiner, "Breakthrough in Organization Development."
27 Argyris, *Interpersonal Competence and Organizational Effectiveness,* p. 281.
28 Shein and Bennis, *Personal and Organizational Change Through Group Methods.*
29 Cooper, Leavitt, and Shelly, eds., *New Perspectives in Organizational Research,* Chapter 4.
30 Shepard and Blake, *op. cit.*
31 Argyris, *Interpersonal Competence and Organizational Effectiveness.*
32 Blake and Mouton, *The Managerial Grid.*
33 Smith, *Managing Geographically Decentralized Companies.*
34 Burck, *The Computer and Its Potential for Management.*
35 Worthy, "Organizational Structure and Employee Morale."
36 Meltzer and Salter, "Organizational Structure and the Performance and Job Satisfaction of Physiologists."
37 Sayles, *Managerial Behavior,* p. 256.
38 Burns and Stalker, *The Management of Innovation.*
   Lorsch and Lawrence, "Organizing for Product Innovation."
   Gouldner, *Patterns of Industrial Bureaucracy.*
   Dalton, *Men Who Manage.*
   Barnes, *Organizational Systems and Engineering Groups.*
   Udy, "Bureaucratic Elements in Organizations."
39 Brown and Shepard, "The Impact of Altered Objectives: Functionalism and Organizational Changes in a Research Laboratory."
40 Guest, *Organizational Change: The Effect of Successful Leadership.*
41 Jaques, *The Changing Culture of a Factory.*
42 McCleery, *Policy Change in Prison Management.*
43 Lawrence, *The Changing of Organizational Behavior.*

Bibliography

Argyris, Chris, *Interpersonal Competence and Organizational Effectiveness*. Homewood: Richard D. Irwin and the Dorsey Press, 1962.

————, *Personality and Organization*. New York: Harper and Brothers, 1957,

Asch, S. E., "Effects of Group Pressure Upon the Modification and Distortion of Judgments," in H. Guetzkow, ed., *Groups, Leadership, and Men*. Pittsburgh: Carnegie Press, 1951.

Barnard, Chester I., *The Functions of the Executive*. Cambridge: Harvard University Press, 1938.

Barnes, Louis B., *Organizational Systems and Engineering Groups*. Boston: Division of Research, Harvard Business School, 1960.

Bell, Gerald D., "Determinants of Span of Control," *American Journal of Sociology*. Vol. 73, 1967, pp. 100–109.

Bennis, Warren G., "Leadership Theory and Administrative Behavior: The Problem of Authority," *Administrative Science Quarterly*, Vol. IV, No. 3, December 1959, pp. 259–301.

Berelson, B., and George A. Steiner, *Human Behavior: An Inventory of Scientific Findings*. New York: Harcourt, Brace and Company, 1964.

Blake, Robert R. and Jane S. Mouton, *The Managerial Grid*. Houston: Gulf Publishing Company, 1964.

Blake, Robert R., Jane S. Mouton, Louis B. Barnes, and Larry E. Greiner, "Breakthrough in Organization Development," *Harvard Business Review*, Vol. 42, No. 6, November-December 1964, pp. 133–155.

Blau, Peter M., *The Dynamics of Bureaucracy*. Chicago: University of Chicago Press, 1955.

————, "The Hierarchy of Authority in Organizations," *American Journal of Sociology*, Vol. 73, No. 4, 1967, pp. 453–467.

———— and J. Richard Scott, *Formal Organizations*. San Francisco: Chandler Publishing Company, 1962.

Bradford, L. P., J. R. Gibb, and K. D. Benne, *T-Group Theory and Laboratory Method: Innovation in Re-education*. New York: John Wiley and Sons, 1964.

Brown, P. and C. Shepard, "The Impact of Altered Objectives: Functionalism and Organizational Changes in a Research Laboratory," in R. Tannenbaum et al., eds., *Leadership and Organization*. New York: McGraw-Hill Book Company, 1961.

Burck, Gilbert, *The Computer and Its Potential for Management*: New York: Harper & Row, 1965.

Burns, Tom and G. M. Stalker, *The Management of Innovation*. Chicago: Quadrangle Books, 1961.

Crozier, Michel, *The Bureaucratic Phenomenon*. Chicago: University of Chicago Press, 1964.

Dalton, Melville, *Men Who Manage*. New York: John Wiley and Sons, 1959.

Emerson, Richard M., "Power-Dependence Relations," *American Sociological Review*, Vol. 27, No. 1, 1962, pp. 31–41.

Fleishman, E. A., E. F. Harris, and H. E. Burtt, *Leadership and Supervision in Industry*. Columbus: Bureau of Educational Research, Ohio State University, 1955.

Fouraker, Lawrence E., unpublished manuscript.

Frank, Jerome, *Persuasion and Healing*. New York: Schocken Books, 1961.

French, J. R. P., Jr., and L. Coch, "Overcoming Resistance to Change," in Dorwin Cartwright and Alvin Zander, eds., *Group Dynamics: Research and Theory*. Evanston: Row Peterson, 1953, pp. 257–279.

———— and Bertram Raven. "The Bases of Social Power," in Dorwin Cartwright, ed., *Studies in Social Power*. Ann Arbor: Research Center for Group Dynamics and Institute for Social Research, 1959.

Glanzer, M. and R. Glazer, "Techniques for the Study of Group Structure and Behavior, II," *Psychological Bulletin*, No. 58, 1961, pp. 1–27.

Gouldner, Alvin W., *Patterns of Industrial Bureaucracy*. Glencoe: The Free Press, 1954.

————, "Organizational Analysis," in Robert K. Merton, Leonard Brown, and Leonard S. Cathrall, Jr., eds., *Sociology Today*. New York: Basic Books, 1959.

Greiner, Larry E., "Antecedents of Planned Organizational Change," *The Journal of Applied Behavioral Science*, Vol. 3, No. 1, 1967.

Guest, Robert A., *Organizational Change: The Effect of Successful Leadership*. Homewood: Richard D. Irwin and the Dorsey Press, 1962.

Guilford, J. P., *Psychometric Methods*. New York: McGraw-Hill Book Company, 1954.

Hall, Richard H., "Professionalization and Bureaucratization," *American Sociological Review*, Vol. 33, No. 1, 1968, pp. 92–104.

Hardin, Einar, "Perceived and Actual Change in Job Satisfaction," *Journal of Applied Psychology*, Vol. 49, No. 5, 1965.

Henderson, L. J., *Pareto's General Sociology*. Cambridge: Harvard University Press, 1935.

Herzberg, F., B. Mausner, and B. B. Snyderman, *Motivation to Work*. New York: John Wiley and Sons, 1959.

Hodgson, Richard C., Daniel J. Levinson, and Abraham Zaleznik, *The Executive Role Constellation*. Boston, Division of Research, Harvard Business School, 1965.

Homans, George C., *The Human Group*. New York: Harcourt, Brace and Company, 1950.

————, *Social Behavior: Its Elementary Forms*. New York: Harcourt, Brace and World, 1961.

Hopkins, Terrence K., "Bureaucratic Authority: The Convergence of Weber and Barnard," in Amitai Etzioni, ed., *Complex Organizations*. New York: Holt, Rinehart, and Winston, 1961, pp. 82–100.

Hovland, C. J., I. L. Janis, and H. H. Kelley, *Communication and Persuasion: Psychological Studies of Opinion Change*. New Haven: Yale University Press, 1953.

Jaques, Elliot, *The Changing Culture of a Factory*. New York: The Dryden Press, 1952.

Katz, Daniel and Robert L. Kahn, *The Social Psychology of Organizations*. New York: John Wiley and Sons, 1966.

Kelman, Herbert, "Compliance, Identification and Internationalization Through Processes of Attitude Change," *Journal of Conflict Resolution*, Vol. II, No. 1, March 1958.

————, "Processes of Opinion Change," *Public Opinion Quarterly*, Spring 1961.

King, B. and I. L. Janis, "Comparison of the Effectiveness of Improvised Versus Non-Improvised Role Playing in Producing Opinion Change," Paper presented before the Eastern Psychological Association, April 1953.

Landsberger, Henry A., "The Horizontal Dimension in Bureaucracy," *Administrative Science Quarterly*, Vol. VI, No. 3, December 1961, pp. 299–332.

Lawrence, Paul R., *The Changing of Organizational Behavior Patterns: A Case Study of Decentralization*. Boston: Division of Research, Harvard Business School, 1958.

———— and Jay W. Lorsch, *Organization and Environment: Managing Differentiation and Integration*. Boston: Division of Research, Harvard Business School, 1967.

Leavitt, Harold J., "Applied Organizational Change in Industry: Structural, Technological, and Humanistic Approaches," in James G. March, ed., *Handbook of Organizations*. Chicago: Rand McNally & Co., 1964.

————, "Applied Organizational Change in Industry: Structural, Technological, and Humanistic Approaches," in W. W. Cooper, H. J. Leavitt, and M. W. Shelly, eds., *New Perspectives in Organizational Research*. New York: John Wiley and Sons, 1964.

————, *Managerial Psychology*. Chicago: University of Chicago Press, 1958.

————, "Unhuman Organizations," *Harvard Business Review*, Vol. 40, No. 4, July-August 1962, pp. 90–98.

Litvak, Eugene, "Models of Bureaucracy That Permit Conflict," *American Journal of Sociology*, Vol. 67, 1961, pp. 177–184.

Loomis, C. P., "Tentative Types of Directed Social Change Involving Systematic Linkage," *Rural Sociology*, Vol. 24, No. 4, December 1959.

Lord, F. M., "Elementary Models for Measuring Change," in C. M. Harris, ed., *Problems of Measuring Change*. Madison: University of Wisconsin Press, 1963.

Lorsch, Jay W. and Paul R. Lawrence, "Organizing for Product Innovation," *Harvard Business Review*, Vol. 43, No. 1, January-February 1965, pp. 109–122.

Mace, C. A., "Satisfaction in Work," *Occupational Psychology*, Vol. 22, 1948.

McCleery, R. N., *Police Change in Prison Management*. East Lansing: Government Research Bureau, Michigan State University, 1957.

McClelland, David C., "Toward a Theory of Motive Acquisition," *American Psychologist*, May 1965.

McGregor, Douglas, *The Human Side of Enterprise*. New York: McGraw-Hill Book Company, 1960.

March, James G. and Herbert A. Simon, *Organizations*. New York: John Wiley and Sons, 1958.

Mayo, Elton, *The Human Problems of an Industrial Civilization*. Boston: Division of Research, Harvard Business School, 1946 (1st published 1933).

Mechanic, David, "Sources of Power of Lower Participants in Complex Organizations," *Administrative Science Quarterly*, Vol. VII, No. 3, December 1962, pp. 349–364.

Meltzer, L. and J. Salter, "Organizational Structure and the Performance and Job Satisfaction of Physiologists," *American Sociological Review*, June 1962, pp. 351–362.

Miller, E. J., "Technology, Territory, and Time," *Human Relations*, Vol. 12, No. 3, pp. 243–272.

Murray, E. J., "A Content Analysis Method for Studying Psychotherapy," *Psychological Monographs*, Vol. 70, 1956.

National Research Council, Committee on Work in Industry, *Fatigue of Workers: Its Relation to Industrial Production.* New York: Reinhold Publishing Corporation, 1941.

Neustadt, Richard E., *Presidential Power.* New York: The American Library, 1964.

Newcomb, T. M., "Attitude Development as a Function of Reference Groups: The Bennington Study," in E. E. Macoby, T. M. Newcomb, and E. L. Hartley, eds., *Readings in Social Psychology.* New York: Holt, Rinehart and Winston, 1958.

Pareto, Vilfredo, *The Mind and Society* (Four Volumes). New York: Harcourt, Brace and Company, 1935.

Parsons, Talcott, *Structure and Process in Modern Societies.* Glencoe: The Free Press, 1960.

Peabody, Robert L., "Perceptions of Organizational Authority," *Administrative Science Quarterly,* Vol. VI, No. 4, March 1962, pp. 463–482.

Pelz, D. C., "Influence: A Key to Effective Leadership in the First-Line Supervisor," *Personnel,* Vol. 29, 1952, pp. 209–217.

———— and Frank M. Andrews, *Scientists in Organizations.* New York: John Wiley and Sons, 1966.

Presthus, Robert, "Authority in Organizations," *Public Administration Review,* Vol. 20, 1960, pp. 88–91.

Rice, A. K., *Productivity and Social Organization: The Ahmedabad Experiment.* London: Tavistock Publications, 1958.

Roethlisberger, F. J., *Management and Morale.* Cambridge: Harvard University Press, 1941.

———— and William J. Dickson, *Management and the Worker.* Cambridge: Harvard University Press, 1939.

Rubenstein, Albert H. and Chadwick J. Haberstroh, eds., *Some Theories of Organization.* Homewood: Richard D. Irwin and the Dorsey Press, 1960.

Rubenstein, Albert H. and H. D. Laswell, *The Sharing of Power in a Psychiatric Hospital.* New Haven: Yale University Press, 1966.

Sargent, W., *Battle for the Mind.* Garden City: Doubleday, 1957.

Sayles, Leonard, *Managerial Behavior.* New York: McGraw-Hill Book Company, 1964.

Schein, Edgar H., *Coercive Persuasion.* New York: W. W. Norton & Company, 1961.

———— and Warren G. Bennis, *Personal and Organizational Change Through Group Methods.* New York: John Wiley & Sons, 1965.

Seashore, S. E. and D. G. Bower, *Changing the Structure and Function-*

ing of an Organization. Ann Arbor: Survey Research Center, University of Michigan, Monograph No. 33, 1963.

Selekman, Benjamin M., *A Moral Philosophy for Management.* New York: McGraw-Hill Book Company, 1959.

Selekman, Sylvia and Benjamin M. Selekman, *Power and Morality in a Business Society.* New York: McGraw-Hill Book Company, 1956.

Shepard, H. R. and Robert R. Blake, "Changing Behavior Through Cognitive Change," *Human Relations,* Vol. 21, Summer 1962, pp. 88–96.

Simon, Herbert A., "Authority," in Conrad Armstrong et al., eds., *Research in Industrial Human Relations.* New York: Harper & Brothers, 1957.

Smith, Geo. Albert, Jr., *Managing Geographically Decentralized Companies.* Boston: Division of Research, Harvard Business School, 1958.

Stein, M. I., ed., *Contemporary Psychotherapies.* Glencoe: The Free Press, 1961.

Strauss, G., "Some Notes on Power-Equalization," in Harold J. Leavitt, ed., *The Social Science of Organizations.* Englewood Cliffs: Prentice-Hall, 1963.

Tannenbaum. Arnold S., "The Concept of Organizational Control," *Journal of Social Issues,* Vol. XII, 1956, pp. 50–68.

———, "Control and Effectiveness in a Voluntary Organization," *American Journal of Sociology,* Vol. 67, 1961, pp. 33–46.

———, *Control in Organizations.* New York: McGraw-Hill Book Company, 1968.

——— and B. Georgopoulos, "The Distribution of Control in Formal Organizations," *Social Forces,* Vol. XXXVI, 1957, pp. 44–50.

Taylor, Frederick W., *Scientific Management.* New York: Harper & Brothers, 1947.

Thompson, James D., *Organizations in Action.* New York: McGraw-Hill Book Company, 1967.

Thompson, Victor A., *Modern Organization.* New York: Alfred Knopf, 1961.

Trist, Eric L. et al., *Organizational Choice.* London: Tavistock Institute of Human Relations, 1963.

Udy, Stanley R., Jr., "Administrative Rationality, Social Setting, and Organizational Development," in W. W. Cooper, H. J. Leavitt, and M. W. Shelley, II, eds., *New Perspectives in Organization Research.* New York: John Wiley and Sons, 1964.

———, "Bureaucratic Elements in Organizations: Some Research Findings," *American Sociological Review,* Vol. 64, 1959, pp. 582–584.

Vroom, Victor H., *Some Personality Determinants of the Effects of Participation.* Englewood Cliffs: Prentice-Hall, 1960.

Walker, Charles R., Robert H. Guest, and Arthur N. Turner, *The Foreman on the Assembly Line.* Cambridge: Harvard University Press, 1956.

Walton, Richard E. and Robert B. McKersie, *A Behavioral Theory of Labor Relations.* New York: McGraw-Hill Book Company, 1965.

Weber, Max, *The Theory of Social and Economic Organization,* translated by A. M. Henderson and Talcott Parsons. New York: Oxford University Press, 1947.

White, Robert and Roland Lippitt, "Leader Behavior and Membership Reaction in Three 'Social Climates'," in Dorwin Cartwright and Alvin Zander, eds., *Group Dynamics: Research and Theory.* Evanston: Row, Peterson, 1933, pp. 585–611.

Woodward, Joan, *Management and Technology.* London: Her Majesty's Printing Office, 1958.

Worthy, J. C., "Organizational Structure and Employee Morale," *American Sociological Review,* Vol. XV, No. 2, April 1950.

Zaleznik, A., *Worker Satisfaction and Development*: Boston: Division of Research, Harvard Business School, 1956.

———, C. R. Christensen, and F. J. Roethlisberger, *The Motivation, Productivity, and Satisfaction of Workers: A Prediction Study.* Boston: Division of Research, Harvard Business School, 1958.

——— and David Moment, *The Dynamics of Interpersonal Behavior.* New York: John Wiley and Sons, 1964.

AUTHOR INDEX

SUBJECT INDEX